DESPERATE
TO BE
NEEDED

BOOKS IN THE **LIFELINES FOR RECOVERY** SERIES

Can Christians Love Too Much?
Margaret J. Rinck
Christian Men Who Hate Women,
Margaret J. Rinck
Desperate to Be Needed, Janet Ohlemacher
Help for the Post-Abortion Woman, Terri Reisser and
Paul Reisser
A *House Divided: The Secret Betrayal—Incest,*
Katherine Edwards
Please Don't Say You Need Me, Jan Silvious
Seeing Yourself through God's Eyes, June Hunt
*Turning Fear to Hope: Women Who Have Been Hurt
for Love,* Holly Wagner Green

Zondervan's **Lifelines for Recovery** series emphasizes healthy, step-by-step approaches for dealing with specific critical issues.

LIFELINES FOR RECOVERY

DESPERATE TO BE NEEDED

FREEING THE FAMILY FROM CHEMICAL CODEPENDENCY

JANET OHLEMACHER

PYRANEE BOOKS

Zondervan Publishing House
Grand Rapids, Michigan

DESPERATE TO BE NEEDED
Copyright © 1990 by Janet Ohlemacher

A Pyranee Book
Published by Zondervan Publishing House,
1415 Lake Drive, S.E., Grand Rapids, Michigan 49506.

Library of Congress Cataloging-in-Publication Data

Ohlemacher, Janet.
    Desperate to be needed / by Janet Ohlemacher.
        p. cm.
    Includes bibliographical references.
    ISBN 0-310-51841-5
    1. Alcoholics—Family relationships. 2. Co-dependence
(Pyschology) 3. Alcoholism—Religious aspects—Christianity.
I. Title.
HV5132.048   1990
362.29′23—dc20   89–49715
                                                              CIP

Printed in the United States of America

90 91 92 93 94 / CH / 10 9 8 7 6 5 4 3 2

CONTENTS

ACKNOWLEDGMENTS 7

INTRODUCTION 9

1. It Isn't Fair 11

2. Flying High, Feeling Low 19

3. Family Heroes, Scapegoats,
   and Lost Children 27

4. "The Enablers"—Prolonging the Agony 33

5. Programs Designed to Help 39

6. Codependents Have Feelings, Too 47

7. Damaged Self-Esteem 55

8. "My Brother's Keeper" 63

9. A "Care"frontation 71

10. Recovery: Healing the Real Hurts 81

11. Choices 91

12. The End Is Just the Beginning 99

ENDNOTES 105

BIBLIOGRAPHY 109

ACKNOWLEDGMENTS

I have to begin by thanking my family and friends, who loved and supported me, wept and laughed with me, and shared the discoveries written in these pages.

I'm particularly grateful to the faculty, staff, and students at Marian College, who positively encouraged my self-esteem and helped make a difference in my life.

Many of the sources quoted here were located by the library staff at Marian College and Manitowoc Public Library. I am deeply indebted to them for their valuable assistance.

I am also indebted to my editor, Nia Jones, and all the staff at Zondervan for having faith in me and for being willing to step out and break the code of silence surrounding codependency. Your assistance has been wonderful!

Most of all, at the heart of the matter, I must praise God, for he made me and gave me the courage to find freedom. AMEN.

INTRODUCTION

I am a sojourner on earth; hide not thy commandments from me
(Psalm 119:19 RSV).

Each one of us is a pilgrim, a sojourner on earth. Each one of us has been given the gift of life, and we are responsible for making that life the best it can be. When we begin the walk, we have no idea where the journey will take us, or when or where it will end. We only know that as sojourners we are temporary residents here.

My story is the story of choices made by one family of sojourners. When my father left my mother, a chemical dependent, I slipped into the role of codependent for a time. But, through a painful process, I learned to accept her as she was, a diseased person who could not come to terms with life. I learned that *her* problem did not make *me* less of a person, and that I could feel my feelings and express them considerately so that I could become the woman God created me to be.

God's Word gives enlightenment, comfort, courage, and guidelines for the most difficult trip. Jesus said, "Do not let your hearts be troubled and do not be afraid" (John 14:27). Through these pages, as you walk out some of the steps in my journey with me, be open to hearing what God has to say to *you*. Believe that the Creator can create you in his image. He did it for me and he can do it for you.

9

1

IT ISN'T FAIR

My mother was an alcoholic. I cannot write a first-hand account of how it feels to be an alcoholic. I cannot even tell you how Mom's alcoholism affected Dad or my two brothers, since each family member's perspective of this problem is uniquely personal.

But I can tell you how Mom's choice to drink excessively impacted my life. And I can tell you that though my experience focuses on alcoholism, the lessons learned apply equally to any chemical dependency.

There was a day when I thought, "It isn't fair!"

For as long as I can remember, my mother drank. I never knew her any other way. As a little girl, I had no idea why Mom behaved the way she did. It was bewildering. For example, one time I was allowed to play with something that on another occasion earned me a sharp reprimand. I didn't know that drinking made the difference in her reaction. Soon, I simply learned to avoid confrontation by being "good."

By the time I was ten, I was telling all my friends that Mom had a serious illness. That got me off the hook when they wanted to come over to play. I just didn't dare let them see Mom in her usual condition.

It was a natural step in the progression, then, to also plead Mom's illness when school functions, programs, and other parent activities came up. In reality, I was covering for her—and for myself.

You see, my mother was an embarrassment to me. She didn't bother to take care of herself. If she did show up at a school function, it was most likely with hair uncombed, clothing disheveled, and without makeup. Weaving to a chair, she might sink into it before she fell, if she was lucky. The humiliation felt worse than the hurt I experienced when she didn't come at all.

After awhile, I began to believe the excuses I made up for Mom. Since I never saw her drinking from a bottle, I couldn't be absolutely certain that was her problem, could I? Nor did I express my feelings about my mother's "illness" to anyone. I wanted to survive.

Survival is the name of the game people play when they live in a dysfunctional family. In addition to the usual ups and downs of living in relationship with others, they must also learn to adjust to one member's chemical dependency (drugs or alcohol)—a condition that alters daily functioning.

Not knowing how to respond to these unpredictable changes, family members develop survival strategies that may be unhealthy or impaired. Instead of one problem, now there are two—the dependency of the alcoholic or drug abuser and the *codependency* of all the family members who allow themselves to be victimized. If not treated, this insidious condition can be just as devastating for those involved as the original dependency.

Toughest of all, codependents become silent partners, and the conspiracy continues unbroken until something happens—a crisis of some kind—when it may be too late to give or receive help. I share my experience because it's the only way to break the awesome code of silence that surrounds the issue of codependency. This "ostrich approach"—burying our heads in the sand and keeping quiet in the hope that the problem will disappear—is the strongest system operative in dysfunctional families. But codependents cannot wish away their problems. Rescue comes only with acceptance of the fact that there *is* a problem.

Family members aren't the only ostriches. I am just as concerned about the apathetic silence from a world that seems unable to face the overwhelming burdens brought on by these dysfunctional families. Statistics prove convincingly that we can no longer afford to ignore these needs.

The stark numbers associated with alcoholism tell only part of the story in chemical dependency. It is commonly understood that nine to ten million American adults and 3.3 million teenagers are alcoholics. Other chemical dependency accounts for another four to five million people. In simpler terms, we're talking about a population the size of New York City and Los Angeles combined.

Still, these may not seem like impressive figures until one remembers that people don't operate in isolation. Each of those eighteen million chemical dependents will interact with a minimum of four others. So, now at least seventy-two million people are affected by those who are chemically dependent. Chances are very good that someone **you know and care about abuses chemicals.**

The impact goes beyond close personal relationships in what an organization called The Other Victims of Alcoholism, Inc. has dubbed the "domino effect."[1]

There are hidden costs which affect all of us. Alcohol and drugs are involved in fifty to eighty percent of all homicides, seventy percent of serious assaults, fifty percent of forcible rapes, and seventy-two percent of all robberies.[2] Criminals who committed these offenses must be housed and fed in jails, so costs begin to spiral.

Nor can we ignore the accidental deaths attributed to drivers under the influence of chemicals. "For the past ten years, at least 26,000 Americans have been killed every year

the domino
effect of
alcoholism
and its
impact on
society

ALCOHOLISM

Alcoholic
Spouse
Children
Parents
Grandparents
In-laws
Employer
Co-workers
Client
Friends

Roommate
Schools
Family Court
Child Neglect/Abuse
Battered Wives
Juvenile Delinquency
Divorces
Welfare Cases
Industry
Unions
Insurance
Criminal Courts
Prisons
Mental Institutions
Hospitals
Government Agencies
Runaways
Professionals
Students
Church

by drunk drivers, who are also blamed for more than
$5 billion per year in medical bills and property damage."[3]

These grim statistics cause us to think. So do unusual
circumstances. Consider this: The helpless and innocent
don't have a choice about being involved in chemical
dependency. What about the unborn child? Continued use of
alcohol, tobacco, and drugs by a pregnant woman decreases
the supply of nutrients to the baby, resulting in risk of
miscarriage, lower birth weight, susceptibility to diseases,
birth defects, and impairment of physical and intellectual
development. Taxpayers have to pick up the tab for these
children—special education programs in schools, specialized
medical services, and long-term care facilities.

And there are many other ways chemical dependency
continues to add up in dollars and cents for the average
citizen:

- Increased medical costs as health fails
- Down time from work as the dependent becomes less
  and less able to perform duties on the job
- Increased numbers of divorced and broken family relationships as the pressures mount
- Greater involvement of social services as dependency
  escalates

Yet the full cost of chemical dependency is almost impossible to estimate. How do you put a price tag on the quality of
life for a family, for example? Even setting aside the medical
expenses, lost earnings, etc., who can measure the cost of
emotional damage, lost self-esteem, and mental anguish?

As a Christian, I've asked God how he could allow
innocent children to pay for something over which they had
no control? I didn't ask to be born the child of an alcoholic.
No, it isn't fair. And it never will be—not for me nor for
anyone else.

Yet this is the reality with which I—and many others—
must live. As the Serenity Prayer says so beautifully, I have

had to learn to accept what I cannot change and have sought the courage to change what I could.

Where do family members find the courage to break out of codependency? In his book, *The Ultimate Secrets of Total Self-Confidence,* Dr. Robert Anthony gives us this insight:

> William James, the eminent philosopher and psychologist, once observed that the greatest discovery of our age has been that we, by changing the inner aspects of our thinking, can change the outer aspects of our lives. Wrapped up in this brief statement is the dynamic truth that we are *not victims but co-creators* in the building of our lives and the world around us. Or, as another sage puts it, we aren't what we think we are, but what *we think*, we are![4]

Over time, I learned to look at my mother through God's eyes, to see her as he sees her. After all, in Luke 6:32–38, Jesus encourages us to love those who are difficult to love:

> If you love those who love you, what credit is that to you? Even "sinners" love those who love them. If you do good to those who are good to you, what credit is that to you? Even "sinners" do that. And if you lend to those from whom you expect repayment, what credit is that to you? Even "sinners" lend to "sinners," expecting to be repaid in full. But love your enemies, do good to them, and lend to them without expecting anything back. Then your reward will be great, and you will be sons of the Most High, because he is kind to the ungrateful and wicked. Be merciful, just as your Father is merciful. Do not judge, and you will not be judged. Do not condemn, and you will not be condemned. Forgive, and you will be forgiven. Give, and it will be given to you. A good measure, pressed down, shaken together and running over, will be poured into your lap. For with the measure you use, it will be measured to you.

All my life I desperately desired a whole family, so much so that I was willing to sacrifice myself to *make* it happen. My mother's alcoholism was a family problem, mine in particular. For a long time, I didn't believe I had any choice. When I became an adult, I continued to act as a codependent because I was thoroughly programmed and didn't know any other way to manage.

I loved my mother, even though she wasn't easy to love. I believed the best way to show her how much was to commit myself to getting her to change. I tried not to judge nor condemn. I even learned to forgive. But my attempts failed. *It didn't work because I had my eyes on the wrong person.* I should have read the rest of the passage (Luke 6:39–42):

> [Jesus] also told them this parable: "Can a blind man lead a blind man? Will they not both fall into a pit? A student is not above his teacher, but everyone who is fully trained will be like his teacher."
>
> Why do you look at the speck of sawdust in your brother's eye and pay no attention to the plank in your own eye? How can you say to your brother, "Brother, let me take the speck out of your eye," when you yourself fail to see the plank in your own eye? You hypocrite, first take the plank out of your eye, and then you will see clearly to remove the speck from your brother's eye.

As I interpret this, I believe it is saying that I can only be responsible for myself. That doesn't mean that I don't care for others. It doesn't mean that the needs of others aren't important to me. It simply means that if I spend as much time focusing on my own development as I do worrying about everyone else, I will achieve the much-desired peace and freedom I'm seeking. Only when I take care of my *log*, will I be able to help others.

2

FLYING HIGH,
FEELING LOW

H ow does an ordinary person like my mother become a chemical dependent? And what happened to the rest of the family when she made that life choice for herself?

In order to understand the implications of codependency, one has to have some knowledge of the process of becoming dependent on chemicals. Researchers point to a variety of reasons for chemical use:

- life stresses, work-related or personal
- crises or major life changes
- fears
- need to be liked
- poor self-esteem
- family history
- genetic predisposition
- socially acceptable—"the thing to do" to have fun

In my quest for understanding I've become aware of other possible medical causes for chemical dependency. Dr. Alan Levin, in citing research done by Dr. Theron Randolph, suggested that alcoholism may be triggered by a food allergy.[1] Gert Behannah, a noted Christian speaker who was herself addicted to alcohol, defines an alcoholic as someone who "has a body allergy and a mental obsession with alcohol."[2]

I can validate some of this research. My body breaks out in a rash whenever I take chemicals. After consulting with an environmental allergist, I discovered that I have a host of hidden food allergies (which explains my cravings for certain foods). It could also explain why others crave beer and alcohol.

While nothing definitive has been made available to the general public, I believe the allergy theory has merit. As silence is broken and more families are willing to provide genetic studies, I believe we will find many valuable new clues to the causes of chemical dependency.

Regardless of the reasons people turn to chemicals, however, problems don't develop until use becomes abuse. A fine line exists between the use of a chemical and its abuse, and experts agree it's different for every individual.

Some key questions need to be asked to help determine whether the line has been crossed into chemical addiction:

1. Does the person using chemicals demand more and more to maintain the effectiveness of the drug?
2. Does abstaining from the chemical produce withdrawal symptoms (nausea, vomiting, irritability, tremors)?
3. Does the person become defensive when someone suggests chemical misuse?
4. Is the person preoccupied with chemicals?
5. Does the person experience behavior changes without any obvious cause?

Psychologists often describe the chemically dependent personality as anxious (often for no reason), defensive, frustrated, angry, emotionally detached, blaming, dishonest, unrealistic, and manipulative. Sounds like someone you know, right? In fact, the chemically dependent person is just an ordinary person who needs chemicals to help cope with everyday life situations.

Addiction generally follows three phases. Initial experimentation with chemicals often produces a pleasant sensation (except for certain drugs like LSD). In Phase 1, the user feels good. If she continues, she may enter a state of euphoria, or a high.

At some point, however, the user loses touch with reality and enters Phase 2. Now, one, two, three, or even four pills or drinks have little effect. The euphoric feeling then becomes painful, and the user loses control. Other people don't find him funny any more. As chemical dependence takes hold, the person may reach for more chemicals, not realizing that a vicious cycle has been set in motion.

In Phase 3, the chemical dependents move toward experiencing the consequences of this behavior. And it is precisely at this point that the roots of codependency are put down. Since dependents don't operate in a vacuum, the persons nearest them are the ones who become the unwitting victims. Ironically, it is the attempt to put a halt to addictive behaviors in a loved one that draws family members into the process. But such concern is seldom rewarded.

On the contrary, when the suggestion is made that the dependent has a problem, the standard response is a defensive one: "Lighten up. Doesn't everyone have an occasional drink or try drugs? I can handle it!"

Unfortunately, this kind of denial starts a chain reaction. As the chemical dependent's behavior moves more and more out of control, the family members who are most concerned may be sucked deeper and deeper into codependent behaviors. Frequently embarrassed in social situations, the family withdraws and becomes isolated and lonely. But this is not the only source of frustration. Confused by traumatic mood swings in the chemical dependent, the family finds internal lines of communication blocked as well. Discussion too often ends in argument, sometimes violent in nature. And while the dependent may not remember later what was said or done, the family has to bear the burden of those memories and may opt to stop talking about the problem altogether.

Desperate to Be Needed

The trap of codependency is fully sprung when the addiction becomes so serious that family members are willing to offer excuses for the chemical dependent, thus "enabling" the person to continue in the addiction. At this point it is very difficult to break the dependency cycle unless a crisis occurs.

A book on crisis counseling defined dependency as "allowing this person, group, or religion to be responsible for their happiness. This includes the luxury of having someone or something to blame whenever failure occurs."[3]

My mother depended on others to meet her needs and to dictate her happiness. The "others" included my father, her children, her family and friends, and her coworkers. If you asked Mom what made her happy, she would almost always respond with a question: "What makes *you* happy?" Her outlook was then based on that person's response to her question. Like a chameleon, the lizard-like creature that changes color to accommodate its environment, Mom simply blended in with her surroundings.

Someone else has said, "Dependency can refer to a state of being, whether physical or psychological; to an attitude and a self-evaluation; to a method of coping and adapting; to a description of a relationship among people; to a mode of living, whether economical, sociological, or psychological, and more."[4]

Dependency itself has its roots in our very beginnings. As infants, we are helpless creatures, dependent on someone else to provide the essentials of life for us. As children, we continue to be dependent, but we learn to flex our independence through healthy stages of development.

Maslow, a noted psychologist, believed that every person starts out with six basic needs: physiological (food, air, water); stimulation (activity, exploration); safety; love and belongingness; esteem (status, careers); and self-actualization. Maslow rated those needs in a hierarchy, beginning with physiological and ending with self-actualization.[5]

To reach self-actualization, one must be physically satisfied, stimulated, safe, loved, and held in esteem. If any of these needs is denied or suppressed, the person cannot develop healthfully.

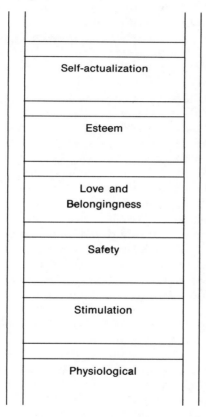

| Self-actualization |
| Esteem |
| Love and Belongingness |
| Safety |
| Stimulation |
| Physiological |

Psychologist William Glasser theorizes that everyone has five basic needs, and he explains them somewhat differently:[6]

1. the need to survive and reproduce
2. the need to belong—to love, share and cooperate
3. the need for power

4. the need for freedom
5. the need for fun

Dr. Glasser further explains that alcoholics (or all chemical dependents) are "dominated by the picture of themselves satisfying all their needs through alcohol [or drugs]. As long as this wonderful all satisfying picture is in their albums, they will drink not only when they are frustrated, but also to prevent future frustration."[7]

He maintains that "replacing the picture can only be done through negotiation and compromise; force will not work."[8] Successful rehabilitation, then, depends on finding and meeting the missing needs.

Codependents also face unmet needs. Robert Subby and John Friel define codependency as "a dysfunctional pattern of living and problem-solving which is nurtured by a set of rules within the family system. These rules make healthy growth and change very difficult."[9]

The prefix *co* means "with or necessary for the functioning of." Because the chemically dependent person doesn't function alone, those closest to that dependent person become sucked into the dependency if they intend to survive in that relationship. So, the family learns an unhealthy mode of operation to meet their basic needs of survival, love and belonging.

Hence, the *sin of silence*. Families don't talk about their problems because talking amounts to admitting that something is radically wrong with the most fundamental system developed to meet needs. So family members become codependent instead.

"Codependency," states Kathy Capell-Sowder, "is an emotional, psychological, and behavioral pattern of coping that is born of the rules of the family and not as a result of alcoholism."[10] That's why codependent relationships are not necessarily connected only with chemical dependency. It's possible for perfectly "normal" families to develop codependent relationships, too.

Melody Beattie, author of *Codependent No More*, defines a codependent as "one who has let another person's behavior affect him or her, and who is obsessed with controlling that person's behavior."[11] As needs are met less frequently or in less healthy ways, family members compromise their value systems by allowing themselves to be affected by the chemical dependent's behavior.

Family members perceive that the chemically dependent person really *needs* them. They make themselves vulnerable by becoming rescuers. They open the door to what I believe develops into a **desperate desire to be needed**, so desperate that the codependents will go to extraordinary lengths to deny their *own* needs in the guise of "helping" someone else. The rescuer becomes a "compulsive helper, someone who cannot keep from stepping in to give aid, even when it is unsolicited."[12]

Hearing yourself described as "compulsive," "stepping in," "interfering," "so desperate for approval that you will actually enable the chemical dependent to continue in an addiction," is far from pleasant. At this stage, codependency mirrors dependency: It is easy to become defensive and deny the truth. Further, it takes real courage and faith to face the facts and recognize the behavior for what they are.

Colette Dowling, author of *The Cinderella Complex*, writes that "dependency, by its very nature, creates self-doubt, and self-doubt can all too quickly lead to self-hatred."[13] Rescuers may begin to hate themselves, thus reinforcing the belief that the addiction (and the codependency) have become vicious cycles that cannot be broken. Rescuers may begin to fear life. When they, too, become victims, the cycle is fully established.

I saw my mother as a dependent person, as someone who very much wanted someone else to take care of her. When my father left home because he could no longer cope with Mom's chemical dependency, I took over the rescuer role as the eldest child. I was ten years old and didn't know any better. I thought Mom needed me.

Not only that, but I needed to survive, to be loved, to belong. I needed to be needed. The best way to guarantee that my own needs would be met was to help my mother. Even though I knew she was sick, I believed she needed me, and I desperately clung to that fact. It gave me my identity.

I didn't know then what I learned later about family roles in chemical codependency: While children cannot completely understand all the dynamics of this kind of family problem, they know only too well that something is wrong and are frequently ready to accept the blame.

Once begun, the bonds of codependency cement quickly and follow a predictable pattern. It *is* possible to break those bonds, but it takes knowledge, acceptance, patience, courage, and faith. After one has accepted the fact that there is a problem, the first step of knowledge involves learning basic family roles and how they operate.

3

FAMILY HEROES, SCAPEGOATS, AND LOST CHILDREN

I recently came across a picture of my younger brother and me. Mom must have had it taken when I was about four and he was three. We looked impishly happy. I'm glad a few joyful moments were recorded, because most of my memories are lost in the fog of forgetfulness or pain.

What is it like being the child of a chemical dependent? I'd say the most accurate answer is, "Living out a nightmare."

Children who are physically abused carry visible scars. Children who are psychologically and emotionally abused also carry scars, but theirs are buried and much more difficult to bring to the surface. Difficult, but not impossible.

The Scriptures paint an interesting profile of an alcoholic in Proverbs 23:29–35:

Who has woe? Who has sorrow? Who has strife? Who has complaints? Who has needless bruises? Who has bloodshot eyes? Those who linger over wine, who go to sample bowls of mixed wine. Do not gaze at wine when it is red, when it sparkles in the cup, when it goes down smoothly! In the end it bites like a snake and poisons like a viper. Your eyes will see strange sights and your mind imagine confusing things. You will be like one sleeping on the high seas, lying on top of the rigging. "They hit me," you will say, "but I'm not hurt! They beat me, but I don't feel it! When will I wake up so I can find another drink?"

Persons using chemicals function in a hazy mist. Incidents may happen they cannot recall. They say and do things that are strange and foreign to their personality. They hurt themselves and can't remember how. Yet they are locked into a strong denial system and will not listen to attempts to make them aware of their problem. They're interested only in the "next drink" or the "next fix."

What happens to the children who live with chemical dependents? Researchers Dr. Stephanie Brown and Claudia Black estimate that ten to sixteen million children under the age of eighteen live in alcoholic homes.[1] While conducting interviews, they found certain consistent feelings among codependent children.

Some children feel the need to control their situations. In an effort to survive, they keep a sharp check on their own emotions. Instead of bringing their feelings to the surface, these children bury them until they feel nothing.

Many youngsters also experience guilt. Children of chemical dependents blame themselves when they see parents abusing alcohol or drugs and believe that things might be different if *they* could somehow change.

I didn't have any trouble identifying with these findings. As a young child I wasn't equipped to handle the overwhelming problems my mother's alcoholism caused, but I operated under the mistaken notion that I was probably somehow to blame and that I'd just have to take over since Mom couldn't help herself. Outwardly silence and retreat were my lines of defense, and I carried these lines right into adulthood. In a sense, I had to be deprogrammed before I could take my place as a normal adult.

Research identifies several key roles played by family members dealing with chemical dependency.[2] First, there are the "**chief enablers**", usually the spouses or persons closest to the chemically dependent person. The chief enablers divide their time between covering for the dependent person and taking the blame for the addict's behavior.

Chief enablers accept responsibility for the dependent by seeing that the person gets to work on time, by calling in sick for him, by making excuses for the embarrassing behavior, and so on. Enablers don't realize that these actions actually prevent the dependent from facing reality.

Chief enablers often take the blame for creating the problems that draw the dependent into chemical use, with some help from the dependent person, of course. Guilt feelings accumulate, and eventually unexpressed feelings are either suppressed, resulting in illness, or they erupt in confrontation. At this point, chief enablers often make a choice. They may join in the chemical use in order to keep peace, or they may confront the chemically dependent person. Depending on how the confrontation is handled, the family finds a solution or disintegrates in divorce.

Children in the family generally fall into three or four other role categories. The "**family heroes**," most often the eldest children, become overly responsible. They appear to be competent and capable and seem to have everything together. That's because the only trust they experience is in themselves. These children work hard, channeling feelings into energy. They do everything humanly possible to please the dependent parent. When they fail, they are left with hidden scars of inadequacy and low self-esteem.

"**Scapegoats**" withdraw from the family, looking to peers for approval instead. Often, these children operate with a defiant, sullen attitude, acting out the deeper feelings inside. Some scapegoats withdraw from reality by becoming chemically dependent later on in life. These children are hiding scars of fear, loneliness, and rejection.

The "**lost children**" in the family also withdraw, but they retreat quietly. They become ultra-independent and aloof, not seeming to need anybody. Lost children often have a weight problem, camouflaging their hidden scars of anger and hurt.

"**Mascots**" develop a humorous, or clownish approach to the overwhelming problems in their life. These children try valiantly to cheer everyone up. They divert attention from more serious matters by doing and saying funny things, often earning themselves a label of hyperactivity. Mascots usually receive the most attention in the family because they demand the most, but they carry scars of insecurity and fear.

How accurate are these descriptions? Surprisingly, these character profiles sound like any normal family. And I suppose there are parallels.

In a normal family, with two observant parents, children receive guidance as they encounter difficulties. The lines of communication are open, and interaction takes place on a regular basis. In my family, however, we practiced absolute silence. We children never talked about anything that bothered us. We knew Mom had problems, but nobody discussed them with us. We developed an unspoken rule that it was best to ignore Mom's behavior. If we didn't talk about it, we didn't have to deal with her drinking.

I felt fortunate in many ways. My mother did not physically abuse us. Considering her condition on many occasions, I would not have been surprised if she had. At least in the beginning, she tried to maintain a semblance of normal family life.

But my father, frustrated after ten years of trying in vain to deal with my mother's complex problems, wanted out. Through the divorce and afterward, my father tried to get custody of my brothers and me. Proving my mother unfit, however, was not easy to do. Like many alcoholics, she was skilled at hiding the evidence. Finally, the judge decided to leave the choice to the children.

As the eldest child, I had to make a no-win decision. Could we continue living with Mom under these difficult conditions? Suppose we were taken away? What would happen to Mom? I sincerely believed that she would die if we left, and I simply couldn't live with that on my conscience. Besides, I had a **desperate desire to be needed**, and Mom needed me.

Not once, not twice, but several times, I insisted that we preferred living with Mom. I never told anyone how I really felt. I, too, was skilled at hiding the evidence, and I had learned to hide my feelings, even from myself. Because nobody knew my fears and thoughts, no one could reassure me or correct my faulty thinking. I thought I was doing my mother a favor. I know now I was wrong.

After my dad left, Mom's condition deteriorated. Soon, she couldn't even get out of bed. Because she consumed only alcohol, she became physically ill. I assumed the role of "family hero" officially. From the age of ten until I turned sixteen, I cooked, cleaned, washed, and cared for my two brothers, Mom, and myself. Nobody else knew the extent to which I covered for Mom.

To compensate for what I lacked at home, I became an excellent student. Several teachers took an interest in me and encouraged me to try harder. I met my needs through work.

Things weren't all bleak, of course. We had a few opportunities to experience real family life. Several weeks in the summer, we spent time with my father and his new wife. Also in the area were my mother's two sisters, and an aunt and grandmother who lived together. Their homes provided the only consistently loving atmosphere we knew. We often found it was very difficult to go back home again.

One might wonder why Mom's family didn't try to force her to seek help. I think there were several reasons. First, of all, we children never discussed the situation with anyone. Since Mom could become very ugly if pinned down, we avoided confrontation by maintaining our strict code of silence.

Further, one of my mother's closest living relatives, herself an alcoholic, refused to accept the facts, even when things got very bad and it appeared evident that I couldn't hold things together any longer, she was reluctant to act. I suppose she found the idea of reliving the past too painful.

For years I was bitter, frustrated, angry, and hurt. That is, until the age of seventeen, when I met someone who drastically changed me and my circumstances. That someone was Jesus Christ.

After my personal encounter with Christ, I began to pray for my mother. I asked for a miracle and, to my great surprise, I got one!

I came home from school one day to find my mother gone. Her family had finally gotten together and arranged for her to be hospitalized. My grandmother came to stay with us, but I don't remember talking about Mom or what was happening to her. To this day, I still don't know how they managed to persuade her to get help.

When Mom came home a month later, she was well. The chemical addiction had been broken. *She* had been treated— but the rest of us were in sad shape.

What happens to codependents in situations like this? Early treatment programs focused exclusively on the chemically dependent person. It is only in recent years that therapists have discovered that treatment will only be successful if the entire network of codependents is also considered.

It was almost predictable, then, that my mother would remain chemical-free only until another crisis struck, and then she would reach back to pull out behavior patterns with which she was most comfortable. As Dr. Glasser pointed out, in Mom's mental picture album there remained a picture of alcohol satisfying her needs, particularly during times of emotional stress. After fifteen years of a peaceful life, all of us were thrust back into the codependency cycle when a crisis erupted. Now we children were adults. Although it took a little longer, those suffocating bonds formed again as if they had never been broken—because they hadn't!

4

"THE ENABLERS"— PROLONGING THE AGONY

For Mom, the crisis began when my aunt died. By that time, I had married my husband, Roger, and we were living in Florida with our three daughters. Mom lived fifteen hundred miles away and worked as a nurse on the night shift. Though free of chemicals, Mom remained a dependent person, and in retrospect I should have realized what effect Aunt Maybelle's death would have on her.

My aunt was a wonderful, caring person, but she never realized that she kept Mom from becoming independent. My aunt had balanced the checkbook, shopped with Mom, sent food home, and taken care of my mother's needs. My aunt was a codependent, with a **desperate desire to be needed**, so she couldn't let go. Mom was all she had.

In talking to Mom over the phone after Aunt Maybelle's death, I couldn't tell that things had changed. Mom seemed so calm and practical, as nurses often are. She fooled me, and not for the first time. I encouraged her to come down for a visit, which she did. She seemed fine to me, and I became convinced that she was handling everything quite well.

So I was completely unprepared for the phone call from my brother Bruce. He told me Mom had fallen and broken her arm getting off a bus. The doctor reported she'd been drunk. My brother was shocked. I was shocked. We were all shocked. I hung up, crying. Mom needed me, whether she knew it or not, and I was determined to rescue her.

People tried to tell me that I couldn't help Mom, but I did not want to listen. Of course I could help. As a codependent, I had a **desperate desire to be needed**, so I had to act on that desire. I just didn't know the best way to accomplish it. Before tackling the problem, I decided to gather up all the information I could, most of which focused on the chemical dependent, not the family members. Again, I could easily see the log in Mom's eyes, but I really was blind to the one in my own . . . .

After reviewing the materials on identifying chemically dependent persons, I read about family roles, as discussed in the previous chapter. I was astounded. How could anyone possibly know what our family picture looked like? They were talking about *us* all right. I very quickly identified the roles my brothers and I had been playing.

As I began to think about and interact more with the information, I encountered the discussion on *enablers*. As I read on, I discovered we had actually enabled Mom to continue her dependency by burying our heads and ignoring the problem. Moreover, I recognized other people—friends and other family members—who had acted as enablers, too. And I was also about to discover that there were professional enablers who could have been instrumental in getting Mom into treatment had they chosen to do so.

I flew home and convinced my brothers to force a confrontation with Mom. Spiritually, I believed it was the right move, and my prayer group supported me while I was on my "mission of mercy."

When we met with Mom, she seemed surprised that we knew about her drinking. After a long and sometimes ugly discussion, she finally agreed to enter outpatient treatment.

Once again, as codependents, we were hooked by our

previously learned behavior patterns. I was elated that Mom was cooperating, not realizing that she would say almost anything to get us off her back. She kept several appointments until the doctors wanted her to take medicine to help her stop drinking. Then she refused, and we moved right back to square one.

Back in Florida, I faced a dilemma. Roger and I considered moving back home to be near Mom. Serious about obeying God's call, we prayed for wisdom and decided to test God by putting our house up for sale. When it sold three weeks later—for cash—we accepted God's call to head north.

Remember now, I was the rescuer, the one stepping in uninvited. I'm quite sure Mom would rather have been left alone. That didn't matter. She needed rescuing. Nothing would deter me from my self-appointed mission.

Just what is an enabler? To refresh the memory, Dr. Johnson describes an **enabler** as "an individual who reacts to the symptom of the illness (chemical dependency) in such a way as to shield the dependent from experiencing the full impact of the harmful consequences of the disease. Thus, the (chemical) dependent loses the opportunity to gain what is needed most, namely, significant insight regarding the severity of the chemical dependency."[1]

Several years later, I've determined that enablers can, but may not necessarily be codependents. Remember, codependents have developed unhealthy patterns of coping with chemical dependency because they have a **desperate desire to be needed**.

Not all enablers become codependents, because they get out before things get worse, but they all do shield the chemically dependent person, usually unintentionally.

I've identified three types of enablers: family, friends, and coworkers or professionals. In understanding how family members unwittingly become enablers, one must review the earlier discussion on how codependency begins. At first, the family enablers see Phase 1 and Phase 2 episodes as isolated incidents. It seems reasonable to excuse what's been happening as something everyone does occasionally.

It also becomes convenient to excuse the behavior. Pressures at school or work caused a temporary need for chemicals, they reason. A crisis touches things off. Family enablers begin to mirror the rationalization of the chemically dependent person.

As the dependency increases, the chemically dependent person begins projecting negative feelings onto the codependent. "You don't really care about me." "Why do you keep nagging—leave me alone!" "You just don't understand . . . ." These are all comments commonly heard in heated discussions.

In the chemical dependent's view, family enablers are the problem. It is then that codependency reaches full bloom. Codependents begin to own the problem and start to feel guilty. If they had some responsibility in causing the dependency, then they should be able to help break it. Hence, the rescuing scenario begins.

At this point, family enablers will go to serious lengths to control the chemical dependency. They'll avoid uncomfortable social situations, hide the chemicals, check up on the chemically dependent person, assume household responsibilities, and if confronted, explain to others why there are mitigating circumstances. They don't want to upset the delicate balance they've achieved by causing more confrontation.

Why do family enablers do that? Why did I do that? I had the false belief that *I* held the key to Mom's problems. First as a child, and then as an adult, I sincerely believed I knew Mom better than anyone and *I* could find a way to help her. It took a very long time and a lot of soul-searching before I could see that I was just as sick as she was.

And it didn't work. **I desperately desired to be needed**, and I felt hurt and disappointed and angry when my attempts to help failed. We succeeded only in digging a bigger and bigger chasm between us, and I felt helpless to stop.

Colette Dowling says "only after she begins to disengage from her belief in her own helplessness can she break out of the vicious cycle of dependency and its brutal effect in her life."[2] When I decided to reach out and get help for myself, I started to break the codependency bonds. A later chapter profiles how that happened, but I think it's important to stress here that *codependency can be broken.* It begins with recognizing the need, continues with gaining knowledge, and eventually leads to action.

As I gained in wisdom and understanding, I decided to seek out other people to assist me in convincing Mom she needed help. Here's where I met the "friendly" enabler and the "professional" enabler.

Mom had a few friends with whom she had developed a close relationship. Some of them were neighbors, and some were people she worked with at the hospital. In approaching them, I was interested in learning two things: how much they knew and how much they were willing to help.

I found out that in this stage of their relationship with Mom, they'd pretty much avoided having any contact with her. Embarrassed by her recent behavior, they chose to avoid seeing her rather than confront her with it.

Mom had no idea that these relationships were strained, so she rationalized their absence by saying, "I don't have time to invite anyone over any more, so they don't invite me," or "Working night shifts puts me on a different schedule from everyone else."

I wasn't too successful in getting help from Mom's friends. They just didn't want to be involved in family problems. They enabled Mom because they refused to help her see how her chemical dependency had ruined their relationship with her.

I then decided to ask Mom's employer the same two questions. Here's where I encountered the "professional" enabler. Her immediate supervisor had been aware of some irregularities, but explained away Mom's erratic behavior. When I offered my own explanation (chemical abuse) and asked for help, he reluctantly agreed to talk to Mom.

Of course, Mom denied she had a problem. I wasn't surprised. But I *was* surprised when her employer refused to press the issue any further. He told me that without specific evidence (only my word) he didn't want to get involved in family problems.

What a blow! The hospital had a connection with a marvelous rehabilitation program. I'd already talked to the counselors there, and they were ready to get Mom started. Why wouldn't her boss cooperate? Didn't he know how vital he was to her recovery?

In the chemical dependent's eyes, a job offers more than financial support. Worthwhile work provides esteem, meeting one of our six basic needs. Loss of esteem is a very effective threat to the chemically dependent person. It breaks into the rationalization process and forces a hard look at reality. When a professional refuses to get involved, that person becomes an enabler.

Since we couldn't expect help from Mom's friends or her employer, we would have to proceed alone. But I refused to give up at this point. I was determined to find some way to help—and I did!

5

PROGRAMS DESIGNED TO HELP

I made another call to the local chapter of the National Council on Alcoholism and took down all the information about programs in the area. We'd already tried crisis counseling and conventional programs, but without success. We needed a way to convince Mom that she needed help.

After driving out to a private program designed to work with alcoholics and their families. I spent several hours with one of their counselors. He presented me with good, if redundant, information about causes of chemical dependency and family roles (see chapter 3). He asked me if I recognized myself in any of these.

I explained that at one time I fit into the pattern he described. I also added that my living faith had taught me how to forgive my mother and forget the past. My concern centered around Mom's present drinking problem.

The counselor suggested that I needed help as much as my mother did. After all, he said, Mom's drinking problem wasn't *my* problem. He felt I needed help in learning how to deal with her. In other words, I should be worrying more about myself than about my mother. In God's words, I should look at the log in my own eyes before I examined the one in hers.

I had a hard time accepting that counselor's theory. I believed that because I cared about Mom, it was my Christian duty to help her any way I could. I didn't see myself in my childhood role any more. I was an adult. I'd broken the walls of silence by talking to Mom and to others about her drinking. I rejected the idea that I should give up trying to help her.

At the close of the session, the counselor congratulated me on my overcoming faith. He seemed amazed that I didn't fit the pattern most other family heroes follow. I hadn't married an alcoholic or become one myself. I enjoyed a healthy relationship with my husband and children. It had taken a while, and needed lots of hard work, but with God's help I had succeeded.

The counselor suggested that I give him a call if I convinced Mom to get treatment, or if I decided I needed help for myself. However, he didn't offer me any ideas about how to convince her. I left with a smaller checkbook balance and a feeling of frustration.

A few weeks later, I heard about a Christian counseling service at a nearby church. I decided to call and make an appointment. I had nothing to lose, and they just might have some answers for me.

I'm very grateful to the counselor I saw there. First, he reassured me that my experiences of healing and forgiveness were very real (these are detailed in chapter 9). He understood the power of Christ's forgiving love.

This Christian counselor agreed, though, that I had made my mother's problem my problem, and he helped me put things into perspective. He advised me to prioritize my difficulties and plan a course of action that would bring *me* relief. While he did offer to meet with me and Mom and help me convince her to seek help, he had to recommend another program for her actual treatment.

Immediately after leaving the church, I drove up to talk to Mom, while I had the courage. I met her just as she was returning home from grocery shopping. We chatted casually for a few minutes when I suddenly noticed something peculiar tucked under the pillow Mom was sitting on. It was the rim of a bottle, just barely visible. The situation seemed so ludicrous, I wanted to laugh.

Something like pity hit me at that moment. Here we were, talking as if nothing was wrong, while my mother sat on her bottle. She knew the bottle was there. Did she really think she could hide it from me?

Something snapped inside me. Maybe I didn't have the right to disturb Mom's little fantasy world. After all, it was her life. She wanted to drink—that was her choice. If she was happy, wouldn't it be kinder and simpler just to leave her alone?

I began to have doubts. Maybe I really did have the problem. I found myself getting hooked into rationalization again. So, instead of approaching Mom about seeing a counselor with me, I talked on for a few minutes longer. And finally, I left. I just didn't have the heart to destroy her happy mood by tackling her drinking.

We continued to play the charade. I decided to settle back and let things rest awhile. And I waited for God to act again.

During the wait I wasn't idle. I continued calling and getting information about local programs. First, I talked to the people at Alcoholics Anonymous. If I couldn't get Mom to go to them, maybe someone would come and talk to her. Yes, they assured me, someone would come—but Mom had to make the call requesting help herself.

This answer infuriated me! The last thing Mom wanted to do was to make that call. How long would I have to wait for her to reach out? I had to do something before she killed herself. Once again, as a codependent, I had a desperate desire to be needed. *What could* I *do?* I asked.

To answer my questions, the A.A. counselor put me in touch with an Al-Anon group. These nondenominational groups are specifically formed for families of alcoholics. Most larger areas have a branch.

Ideally, they provide a place to share the frustrations and difficulties faced by family members. Following guidelines similar to A.A., they stress Christian principles in twelve steps, urging family members to concentrate on their own behavior and not the alcoholic's. Group support encourages the family members to try different ways to minimize the alcoholic's influence on the family.

The following excerpt from the Al-Anon information tract gives a more detailed explanation:[1]

> The Al-Anon Family groups are a fellowship of relatives and friends of alcoholics who share their experience, strength, and hope in order to solve their common problems. We believe alcoholism is a family illness and that changed attitudes can aid recovery.
>
> Al-Anon is not allied with any sect, denomination, political entity, organization, or institution; does not engage in any controversy, neither endorses nor opposes any cause. There are no dues for membership. Al-Anon is self-supporting through its voluntary contributions.
>
> Al-Anon has but one purpose: to help families of alcoholics. We do this by practicing the Twelve Steps, by welcoming and giving comfort to families of alcoholics, and by giving understanding and encouragement to the alcoholic.

Unfortunately, I lived in a small community, and the nearest city was too far away for me to travel for weekly meetings. One of my brothers did join an Al-Anon group later, which proved very helpful.

However, I cannot stress enough the importance of loving support in a crisis. For years, I had been part of a prayer group in Miami and found it easy to share my deepest feelings with fellow Christians, who supported me with love and prayer. Working through rough times, it really helps to have caring people around you.

Several years ago, I became aware of a new support group called Alcoholics Victorious.[2] They base their creed on

2 Corinthians 5:17. With the power of Christ, an alcoholic (or chemical dependent) can be victorious in overcoming chemical dependency.

I recently learned of another support organization: The Other Victims of Alcoholism, Inc.[3]

Many of the publications cited were produced by a company called Health Communications, Inc., which publishes educational materials relating to the field of chemical addiction (see bibliography for more information). Through them, I discovered the Hazelden Foundation.[4] They conduct research, provide workshops, and publish an excellent newsletter for health care professionals. These and others are beginning to make a dent in increasing public awareness of chemical dependency.

I continued my search by checking further into one of the programs recommended for family treatment. I found out how the program operates and the details of committing a chemically dependent person. A client signs in for thirty days, spending the first three or four days in a detoxification unit of a hospital to work off the effects of the chemicals.

Then the patient moves to a ward. Group and individual therapy sessions are scheduled as part of the treatment. These sessions bring the chemically dependent person into accountability for the condition. When the chemical dependent is ready to return home, the after-care program for families continues for two years or more.

Costs vary, depending on how the hospital receives its funding. The average private program ranges from $5,000 to $8,000. Many insurance companies now recognize the need for family care and will cover at least part of the cost. County and state-operated programs also reduce the cost for those persons who have limited funds.

All these programs remain ineffective, however, unless the chemically dependent person takes the initiative in signing up. My problem was getting Mom there. In asking "How?" I got every answer from "I don't know" to "Drag her there!"

What now? I tried calling the National Council on Alcoholism again for some new ideas. The young woman on the phone suggested I read *I'll Quit Tomorrow* by Dr. Vernon Johnson. It might be my answer, she said.

I ordered the book from her, and when it arrived I couldn't put it down. At last someone spoke a language I could understand! In his book, Dr. Johnson points out that families don't have to wait until things are impossible before taking action. I finally had hope!

Dr. Johnson outlined a procedure called "family intervention."[5] This process is used successfully at his hospital in Minneapolis, Minnesota, where the commitment rate is seventy-five percent. Recalling that I had read about Betty Ford's family having tried something similar, I became very excited. Here was a proven technique that had received national attention.

I got busy inquiring about the availability of such a program in our area. Since I now knew what to ask for, getting an answer was much simpler. Although the technique was fairly new, at least one hospital practiced intervention in encouraging chemically dependent people to reach out for the treatment they need.

The best time to try an intervention, recommended Dr. Johnson, comes during a crisis. The chemical dependent, already under outside pressure, responds better at this time. It's easier to cut through the defenses. When my mother had a crisis, and she would, we needed to be prepared to reach her.

Since I didn't have to act immediately, I took my time and prayerfully sifted through the information. I also talked things over with my brothers. Their cooperation would be vital to a successful intervention. At that time, I had no idea how close we were to a crisis.

A month later, on New Year's Day, I received a call from my mother's employer. The night before, she had arrived at work smashed. He had fired her on the spot and thought I'd like to know. His enabling came to a bitter end.

Well, we had our crisis. Without a job, Mom would lose her esteem, not to mention her only income. We already knew her health was precarious. What would she do now?

The timing gave us a perfect opportunity for an intervention. We had a choice—intervene now or perhaps never.

6

CODEPENDENTS HAVE FEELINGS, TOO

W hen I made my first appointment to meet with the intervention team, I was apprehensive. I had some ideas about what to expect, but I also sensed that God was about to reveal something that would change my life.

I met first with Bill, who would serve as team leader. He outlined the procedure we would follow. Even though friends and employers would not help us, Bill assured me that children are often the most effective confronters, and I was confident my brothers would help.

Next, we were instructed to make a detailed list of specific incidents we had witnessed. Bill encouraged us to avoid general statements like: "You always . . . ." or "You never . . . ." and stick to facts: "You fell down . . . ." or "You broke the lamp . . . ."

He also encouraged us to make "I" statements and attach feeling words to the incidents.

I encountered a major problem here. When Bill asked us to write down how we felt about my mother's drinking, I couldn't find the words to express my feelings. I knew vaguely that living with an alcoholic was like living out a nightmare, only you know it's for real. But I couldn't think of any feeling words that I could attach to specific examples of Mom's drinking, for one very good reason.

When I came to know Jesus as my personal Savior, I invited him to come in and heal the wounds of my earlier years (see chapter 9). Now, I believed that I could not recall the events or my feelings about them.

However, as I began to reflect later on what I'd been asked to do, God revealed to me that I really wasn't in touch with my feelings. If I wanted to be honest, and I did, I needed to get in touch with the child inside.

I know now that as a codependent, I had suppressed my real feelings for so long that I was locked into a habit I couldn't break. Even as an adult, I blocked my feelings. If my mother was a chameleon—someone who changed her opinions and feelings to match the person with whom she was interacting—I, as a codependent, was guilty of the same thing.

Now I needed to understand how and why I suppressed my feelings. The roots of my behavior had their beginnings in infancy.

H.F. Harlow, an animal psychologist, has experimented in behavior, using monkeys. A group of infant monkeys received nourishment from a cold, wired machine. Then they were set down with a warm, soft terrycloth "mother," who supplied no nutrients but provided warm contact. After a time, when given a choice, the baby monkeys preferred the cuddly apparatus, even though it didn't feed them.

Harlow continued studying the animals' behavior. Those who received only food, shelter, and heat but had no contact with the other monkeys became cold and antisocial when returned to the others. After six months, though, their behavior reversed. Those left alone for more than a year never changed.[1]

These experiments provided valuable information about how humans develop. Psychologists now agree that deprived children experience similar problems in their development.

"The dependency period of an infant is crucial—crucial, that is, in the development of a person who loves and is lovable, who has emotions and relationships, and is capable of altruism and hope."[2]

"The first year, the child is an aware fetus who, while helpless to act, is not helpless to perceive, and with that perception is learning lessons he will never forget."[3]

We mistakenly believe that children are too young to remember what's happening around them, but they aren't. We think that children are resilient and will recover from trauma, but without help they don't. We assume children think logically and will therefore correctly discern what's wrong in their circumstances, but they aren't developmentally capable of this until they're much older.

Like physical growth, our emotions, mental ability, and spirituality mature in given stages. From day one of birth, we store impressions in our mental computer banks. Unless we consciously dig out the old information from time to time and replace it, we can expect troubles to pop up.

In a pamphlet for the Narramore Christian Foundation entitled "Damaged Emotions,"[4] David A. Seamands commented, "First, the Christian may severely repress his inner problems, crush them the moment they show themselves— both inwardly and outwardly. Far from facing them and trying to resolve his problems, he denies they even exist and they are driven deep within himself, not to lie dormant; rather to reappear in disguised form."

As a codependent, then, I'd experienced trauma as the child of a chemically dependent person. I didn't know it, but my memory bank held things I had suppressed. I had learned to deny my feelings because it was far more painful to experience them.

Because I suffered from inconsistent and inappropriate love and punishment, I became confused. I believed that *my* actions caused Mom to get angry. As a child, I didn't know that other things beyond my control were responsible for Mom's anger, and my behavior just put it into focus for her.

In time, I felt deeply guilty for making her angry. I also felt guilty because I believed that my behavior caused Mom to drink. Nothing I did ever seemed good enough. I became a perfectionist because I wanted so much to please her.

I had no idea that what I did really didn't matter. Mom herself denied feelings, and her needs were so great that nothing I could do would ever satisfy them. I didn't know that because I couldn't discuss it with anyone—the sin of silence I've mentioned earlier. The end result of denial is the suppression of the truth.

In the progression of the disease of chemical dependency, denial turns into delusion. One begins to believe that things will get better. "If I try hard enough . . . ." or "If I'm good enough . . . ." Delusion also prevents codependents from seeing the reality of the situation.

As conditions worsen, fearful feelings develop. "What if someone finds out and takes us away?" "What if Mom hurts herself?" "Who will take care of her if I'm not around?" These are all real fears for children. Most of all, codependents fear they will lose control.

How does that translate into action? The codependent becomes afraid to try anything new. It's best to cling to what is known because the unknown may be frightfully worse.

When tightening the controls doesn't work, a sense of hopelessness sets in. It doesn't take much to move into depression from here. Deep inside, angry feelings surface. "Why is this happening to me?" "How could she do this to us?" "Why can't he see what he's doing to himself?" The codependent now reaches the gravest danger point—the temptation to abuse chemicals as a way of releasing pent-up feelings.

As David Seamands said, the dormant repressed feelings begin to reappear in distinguishable forms. The codependent often develops headaches or stomach problems or some other physical ailment seemingly unrelated to any physical cause. For me, my repressed emotions manifested themselves as allergic reactions.

Please understand, repressed feelings don't cause illnesses, but they magnify them. It took me a long time to accept this. Things that don't normally make me break out will trigger hives when I'm under stress.

Because the chemically dependent person is locked into a private world of unmet needs, that person can't offer the support and encouragement the codependent needs. Feelings of not being good enough, if not rooted out, will lead to feelings of inferiority and supersensitivity.

As a child in school, it was easier to see how that worked. If all the students in class wrote one paper, I *had* to write two. If everyone else used five resources, I *had* to use ten. I always had to do more to prove to myself that I was better—or at least as good as the rest of the kids.

It was harder to detect in relationships, but as a child I picked friends nobody else wanted. We shared a common bond of not feeling good enough.

Fearing to own my feelings, much less express them, I pretty much remained a loner. I couldn't trust anyone. Grown ups had failed me and I had no hope of things getting better.

Colette Dowling defined what she called the Cinderella complex as "a network of distorted attitudes and fears that keeps women in a half-light, retreating from the full use of their minds and creativity. Like Cinderella, women today are still waiting for something external to transform their lives."[5]

I hated to admit it, but that described me to a "T." I sat in the cinders of my life, writing down the painful events and my emotions, waiting for someone else to rescue me.

As a Christian, I looked for Jesus to save me. I wanted him to come and change the painful circumstances. I didn't know that the ability to change was within *me.* "Who shall separate us from the love of Christ? Shall trouble or hardship or persecution or famine or nakedness or danger or sword? . . .

No, in all these things we are more than conquerors through him who loved us" (Rom. 8:35–37).

In the book *Victims No More*, Thomas McCabe offers an ABC model that helps to explain how emotional reactions begin. "Before a person experiences an emotion (C), he or she goes through two preliminary steps (A & B) which lead to the feeling."[6]

He goes on to describe Step A as an actual event, person, or object one sees, hears, smells, tastes or touches. In Step B, one makes a judgment or interpretation of the activity or situation. In Step C, one experiences an emotional reaction.

I find that it's very difficult for people to separate the actual sensory data from their evaluation of it. I'm reminded here of an example that came up in a lesson I'd been teaching on effective messages in communication.

As an example of a sensory statement, one of my students came up to me and said, "I see you're not a smoker." I replied that I wasn't, but I also pointed out that she really had made an evaluative statement. She couldn't assume I wasn't a smoker without giving me some sensory data (Step A). So, I helped her out. What she "saw" was that I chose to sit in a non-smoking section of the cafeteria, that I didn't reach for a cigarette after lunch, that she didn't smell tobacco on my breath or clothes, and that my teeth weren't stained; she therefore interpreted correctly that I didn't smoke (Step B). Depending on her emotional feeling about smoking, then, I was okay or not okay (Step C).

In communicating effectively, then, I see something (or hear, smell, taste, touch); I evaluate what I see, and then I react with a conclusion or an emotion. As an adult facing codependency for a second time, I realized I was seeing, evaluating, and reacting with many of the same feelings I'd used as a child.

I wanted to deny what my eyes saw because it was painful. I wanted to delude myself into believing it couldn't be. I wanted to put another interpretation on the actual facts. I still had a **desperate desire to be needed**, only I didn't know what that was.

I couldn't accept it then, but my damaged emotions had contributed to a lack of self-esteem, denying one of the six basic needs of every human being. My **desperate desire to be needed** supplanted my self-esteem and continued to prevent me from actualizing what I really wanted: healthy, whole personhood. In order to begin walking down the healing road to recovery, I had to identify and attach feelings to all the events I'd experienced.

So, I began my list, and I put it into the following framework:

May, 1982   Mom stood at her door, giggling, and refused to unlock it. I felt angry and embarrassed because my children were with me and didn't understand why Grandma was acting so funny.

June, 1982   I called Mom fifteen times today and she didn't answer, though I knew she was there. I felt deeply anxious, fearing something had happened, so I called the neighbors. Then I felt ashamed and embarrassed when the neighbor found Mom in a drunken stupor.

As I made out my list and started adding up my feelings, I realized that part of my past was indeed coming back to haunt me. I felt those old feelings of inadequacy return, and I knew then I had to deal with them now, as an adult, or I would never be free.

From teaching communication skills, I know that there's no such thing as a "bad" feeling. Feelings aren't right or wrong; they just exist. The scared little girl who lived inside me would just find another hiding place unless I took steps to bring her out into the light. I needed healing for my damaged self-esteem.

7

DAMAGED SELF-ESTEEM

What is self-esteem? Self-esteem, used interchangeably with self-worth, self-image, and self-acceptance, describes the way we think and feel about ourselves.

What determines self-esteem? "How we feel about ourselves depends largely on our response to the 'feedback' we have gotten from the important people in our lives. If these 'significant others' have helped us feel important and loved, we will be inclined to have a positive self-image. If they have given us reason to feel inadequate and unneeded, then we are apt to think we're a failure, we have nothing to offer, we don't like the way we look, and we doubt that anyone could love us."[1]

What are the characteristics of someone with damaged self-esteem? These people constantly blame others or complain and find fault with everything. They need lots of attention.

Usually people with damaged self-esteem lack close friends. They have an aggressive need to win at all costs. Selfish and somewhat greedy, they overindulge in food, most likely abuse chemicals, often suffer from depression, and may be suicidal.

Damaged self-esteem results in indecisiveness. These

people often procrastinate. They will put up a false front to hide perceived inadequacies. If left unchecked, damaged self-esteem locks them into a negative way of life that's extremely difficult to change.

What damages one's self-esteem? At least three causes are generally accepted as inflicting permanent damage on self-esteem. The first comes from negative beliefs and values voiced by parents and significant others. The second stems from repeated put-downs and distorted comments made by peers and teachers, and perceived from such things as grades, I.Q. tests, and other analytical instruments.

Third, self-esteem can also be damaged by a negative religious, moral, or ethical philosophy, particularly one that emphasizes unworthiness and/or guilt. Just as young children are vulnerable to what they see and hear at home, they are also vulnerable to what they see and hear at church. If the only concept being preached is "You're not good enough," children absorb that, and it reinforces negative information they've already received from other sources.

Once developed, why does a person sustain a damaged self-esteem? Shouldn't adults know better? Dr. Dan Kiley, author of *The Wendy Dilemma*, suggests that "negative self-esteem sustains itself not only because changing it calls for new attitudes and behaviors, (and change is difficult), but also because to give it up, a person must get rid of self-pity, and when self-pity goes, the person loses the self-soothing that goes with it."[2]

The adult inside me knows that, rationally speaking, I'm okay. The child inside me contradicts that, however. The child within says, "Something's wrong with me. I can't do anything right."

If I want to stop coloring my perception as always wrong, I have to erase my child's picture and draw another one. "Poor self-confidence is simply a problem of awareness. Once you are aware of the truth about yourself, you will be able to understand why you are the way you are and learn to love and accept yourself."[3]

What is the truth about myself? I am the child of a chemically dependent person. I am a codependent. I understand what caused me to become a codependent in this relationship and how my feelings of inadequacy formed. I can break those bonds and restore my self-esteem, but I need help. And I look to God to provide me with that help.

All throughout the New Testament, Jesus spoke about loving one's own self. In **Matthew 22:39, he said: "Love your neighbor as yourself." Jesus knew that we could never learn to love anyone until we learned to love ourselves first.**

In order to love myself, I had to see myself as God saw me. In other words, I needed to put on his eyeglasses for a while and see things from *his* perspective.

God created every one of us and knows us well. Psalm 139:13–16 says:

> For you created my inmost being; you knit me together in my mother's womb. I praise you because I am fearfully and wonderfully made; your works are wonderful, I know that full well. My frame was not hidden from you when I was made in the secret place. When I was woven together in the depths of the earth, your eyes saw my unformed body. All the days ordained for me were written in your book before one of them came to be.

In Luke 12:7, Jesus said, "Indeed, the very hairs of your head are all numbered. Don't be afraid; you are worth more than many sparrows." God knows me and he loves me.

> Therefore I tell you, do not worry about your life, what you will eat; or about your body, what you will wear. Life is more than food, and the body more than clothes. Consider the ravens: They do not sow or reap, they have no storeroom or barn; yet God feeds them. And how much more valuable you are than birds!" (Luke 12:22–24).

Desperate to Be Needed

So, God asks me to trust him. Jesus goes on to say that God knows my needs. He tells me to seek his kingdom and what I need shall be mine. So why do I worry?

"Adult children of alcoholics [and chemical dependents] overreact to changes over which they have no control," says Dr. Janet Woititz, author of *Adult Children of Alcoholics.* "They constantly seek approval."⁴ I did that. I overreacted to changes, particularly when I had no say over them. I was afraid to trust, to take risks. And even my boss perceived that I needed constant approval.

Why do codependents behave that way? Dr. William Glasser tells us: "We are willing to pay the price of these painful behaviors because they provide control."⁵

Losing control frightened me. I didn't even trust God because I didn't want to surrender control even to him. There is hope, however. "Man, alone among animals, is created incomplete but with the capacity to complete himself."⁶ God created us with the freedom to make choices.

The first step in restoring self-esteem is to surrender ourselves to God. Over and over, the New Testament reminds us that it is only by dying, or surrendering, that we are free to achieve God's highest purpose. Jesus said, "I tell you the truth, unless a kernel of wheat falls to the ground and dies, it remains only a single seed. But if it dies, it produces many seeds. The man who loves his life will lose it, while the man who hates his life in this world will keep it for eternal life" (John 12:24–25).

Jesus also said, "If anyone would come after me, he must deny himself and take up his cross and follow me. For whoever wants to save his life will lose it, but whoever loses his life for me will find it" (Matt. 16:24–25).

Profound thoughts, aren't they? Paradoxical, too. One might believe that this would justify the self-sacrifice that codependents make. But losing your life by following God and losing it by allowing it to be swallowed up in someone else's life are two different things.

58

Relinquishment—that's the key word to restoring self-esteem. I need to let go of my old, destructive codependent self and entrust it to God. I need to seek the answers within myself as God reveals them to me.

"The self continually evolves, continually shapes itself, continually affects the way it is experienced—by the continuing stream of choices and decisions it makes in the course of living. That is why change and growth are possible. We are not obliged to remain the prisoners of yesterday's errors, or yesterday's defaults on the responsibility of appropriate consciousness."[7]

The way I choose to deal with reality either strengthens my self-esteem or weakens it. I have a choice in the matter. God gave me that choice.

Let me give you an example. I worked as the head of public relations for a library. Part of my job involved sending out news releases giving information about library programs.

Occasionally, the wrong information went out. If I had low self-esteem, I would have said to myself, "That's right. You never pay any attention to details. You always get things wrong," and I'd react by being angry with everyone around me for no apparent reason. The negative responses reflected from others would further weaken my self-esteem.

If I had a higher self-esteem, I would have said, "So you made a mistake. You'll make others. What do you need to do to correct this?" and I'd go about my business without making a fuss.

To develop a higher self-esteem, one needs to surrender the old damaged self-esteem to God and replace it with a vision of the child he created. This requires making a conscious and deliberate effort, and it takes lots of time and practice. It involves being willing to change.

Dr. Robert Schuller writes, "Perception is a mirror. How you see God will depend a great deal on how you see yourself. Angry people either don't believe in God or believe in an angry God. On the other hand, loving people believe in God and believe in a loving God."[8]

Look in a mirror and really take a look at yourself. What do you see? An angry person, a sad person, a happy person, or a bitter one? Are you pleased with what you see? Remember, perception is like a mirror—it only reflects back what is actually there.

I first encountered this concept when I came to know Jesus personally twenty-five years ago. He asked me to look in the mirror. I didn't like what I saw! No wonder other people didn't respond to me, either.

As I looked longer and longer, I realized that what I saw in the mirror reflected the "me" inside. I *was* angry. I *was* bitter. I felt hopeless, and it showed—in the droop of my stance, in the expression in my eyes, in the dullness of my hair, in my countenance. The giant log of my despair sat on my shoulder, and I could see it weighing me down.

God spoke to me then through the story of his own Son's life. He pointed out how the beauty of his grace could make me beautiful. When I asked how to receive that gift, he told me I couldn't earn it or buy it. I could never be good enough for it, either. It was a *gift*. God gave his Son so that I might live and become his child, too.

There was only one catch. I had to accept the gift. I had to make my choice, and I did.

In choosing to see myself as a child of God, a daughter of the King, I began to put to death my damaged self-esteem and replace it with the vision of what God had created in me. With the help of his Holy Spirit, I slowly began to erase the tattered image and put a new one in its place.

As I worked through my lists and identified my emotions regarding Mom's chemical dependency, I began to identify my own unmet needs. Understanding how I came to be was only a stepping-stone to finding out who I really was.

As I put together the pieces of my personality through the years, I discovered that God had given me a wonderful sense of humor; I was warm and tender-hearted. I had a lovely smile, and I enjoyed an impish streak that could help me take risks. I discovered I made a good teacher because I genuinely cared for others.

As a part of seeing reality, however, I also became aware of my flaws. I was a codependent. I had a **desperate desire to be needed.** I had developed unhealthy ways to meet that basic need.

But God wasn't finished with me yet. There were days when I experienced deep despair, when I thought I'd never see the end of all this searching. Those were the days when he would send Bible verses to comfort and strengthen me.

I thought of Jesus and his disciples, who were so downcast at the thought of his leaving them. Yet he quietly reassured them they knew not the Father's plan, and he promised that he would never leave them alone but would provide the Holy Spirit to remain with them forever.

When the days seemed darkest to me and the future looked bleak, God's Word spoke to me:

> We are hard pressed on every side, but not crushed; perplexed, but not in despair; persecuted, but not abandoned; struck down, but not destroyed. We always carry around in our body the death of Jesus, so that the life of Jesus may also be revealed in our body (2 Cor. 4:8–10).

When I replaced my picture of damaged self-esteem in my memory album, I put God's picture of hope in its place. God made me, and I was okay. I didn't need anyone else to tell me that good news!

How much we are loved doesn't depend on how much we can do but on who we are. I am a survivor. I care about others. I learned valuable lessons because I *wanted* to learn them. I share what I've learned because I think I can help open the door to light for others. "Ask and it will be given you; seek and you will find; knock and the door will be opened to you" (Matt. 7:7).

Desperate to Be Needed

As my search for truth continued, I had to look at the impact my codependency had on the others around me. Just as the chemically dependent person doesn't operate in a vacuum, neither does the codependent. Codependency also impacts family relationships, friends, and coworkers. To effectively break the chains of codependency, I had to examine the effect that change would have on all my other relationships.

8

"MY BROTHER'S KEEPER"

F amilies of chemically dependent people learn to play games to keep the relationship from falling apart. "A game consists of a series of behavior interchanges between at least two people. The purpose of these interchanges is to avoid intimate and legitimate exchanges of feelings. They offer a non-threatening way for people to pass time together."[1]

One of the first games families of chemical dependents learn to play is a nonverbal one I'll call "Let's Pretend." "Let's Pretend that Daddy's behavior doesn't bother us." "Let's Pretend Mom is really a wonderful, warm person." "Let's Pretend" is a form of denial and delusion. We don't have to deal with something if we pretend it doesn't exist.

Another game families play is "Let's Be Silent." "Let's Be Silent about what happened because it won't happen again." "Let's Be Silent about what we saw because it will only end in an argument." "Let's Be Silent" feeds off the sense of hopelessness families develop as they try to understand what's going on as the chemical dependency gets worse.

"Let's Argue" is yet another game. Confrontation occurs after unexpressed angry feelings have been stuffed down inside until there's no more room. "Let's Argue" starts out as verbal abuse but, if allowed to continue, may become physical.

Constant arguing leads to "Let's Blame." In this game, family members look for someone else on whom to fix the responsibility for their actions. "Let's Blame grandpa because he drank a lot, too." "Let's Blame the job because it isn't easy being an executive or a dock worker." "Let's Blame" takes the heat off the dependent for a while.

"Pity Party" is a session where family members seek someone out to listen and feel sorry for them. They don't want answers at a "Pity Party"; they just want to feel sorry for themselves.

Chemically dependent people hook their families into games to avoid or delay confronting the real issue: chemical abuse. Talking about "the problem" threatens the dependent's neatly wrapped up world because it means that someone is going to have to change.

Family members who develop codependent behaviors become very good at playing the games. When children who have been brought up in chemically dependent families grow up and seek marriage partners, they often have problems.

Codependent children have been taught to avoid feelings. They've developed a damaged self-esteem. They've put up barriers so no one will get really close. It's very difficult for codependent children to establish positive relationships because they didn't have good role models to follow.

It's not surprising, then, that statistics indicate fifty to seventy-five percent of codependent children either become chemical abusers themselves or they marry someone who's chemically dependent. Because they have a **desperate desire to be needed**, they seek out a needy person as a marriage partner. Without a conscientious effort, they are unable to break the codependency bonds.

True love requires commitment and sacrifice. To establish a healthy communication system that allows the exchange of need-sharing, the two partners have to take risks. Codependents don't take risks because it might cause them to lose control.

Dr. James Dobson has provided some valuable insights into the causes and effects of marital disharmony. He believes that "the problem has its origins in childhood, long before a young man and woman stand at the altar to say 'I do.' For her part, the girl is subtly taught by her culture that marriage is a lifelong romantic experience; that loving husbands are entirely responsible for the happiness of their wives; that a good relationship between a man and woman should be sufficient to meet all needs and desires; and that any sadness or depression that a woman might encounter is her husband's fault. At least, he has the power to eradicate it if he cares enough."[2] It's just not a realistic picture.

Dobson goes on to point out that men learn some misconceptions, too. Men believe that their job is to provide materially for the family. They're expected to become successful to maintain an assumed standard of living. Paying the bills and showing loyalty are the most women should expect from them—more unrealistic pictures.

For the codependents, whose concept of reality has already been distorted by the games played as children, loving relationships may be downright impossible to sustain. Dobson indicates that marriage partners need to dialogue about their preconceived ideas of marriage. Given the inability to express feelings appropriately, their damaged self-esteem, the need to maintain control at all costs, and the **desperate desire to be needed** that will push them to any lengths to rescue someone else, codependent marriages seem doomed before they begin.

I give God the credit that I didn't marry a chemically dependent person, nor become one myself. Because I developed a close personal relationship with God and came to love and accept myself *before* I married, I broke the codependency bonds early.

This wasn't done overnight, however, and it wasn't easy. I suffered from the effects of codependency until I learned what it was and how to change.

I'm fortunate that my husband has a compassionate, compromising nature. I'm sure there were times when my behavior frustrated him no end. Many other men might have given up, but Roger's tenacity kept him probing and pushing until we both found compromises with which we could live.

Dr. Robert Schuller says, "The really strong persons are those who have self-denial at the core of their love. They are people who can give themselves freely. They know how to go more than half-way. They can compromise when the going gets rough. For compromise is self-denial, it is backing down, backing off, and settling for less in the present moment to gain more in the end. Compromising is lowering yourself only to be lifted."[3]

Codependents, who **desperately desire to be needed**, practice self-denial in an unhealthy way. Codependents cannot afford to lose control, so they cannot compromise. It's all or nothing. Unable to see the reality of the picture, they cannot settle for less than winning at all costs. The constant struggle chokes the marriage.

If one's self-esteem is healthy or has been repaired, one can then afford to admit mistakes and become open and honest. Breaking the bonds of codependency allows the person to get in touch with reality and real needs. Healthy communication can then be established. Through the use of "I" messages, the codependent can now stop playing games and start taking ownership of decisions.

When a codependent chooses to stop behaving as a codependent, that can produce problems in the relationship. It feels scary to stop obeying that **desperate desire to be needed**. The codependent needs the support of the spouse at this time. The world enlarges as the codependent no longer "needs" just that dependent person. Continuing to let go leads to increased self-esteem and ultimately the integration of the codependent's true self.

How are the children of codependents affected by these negative behaviors? Parents who cannot communicate, share feelings, or let a spouse get close will not do any better with children. It is a false assumption that maternal/paternal instincts will just take over. Codependents have learned unhealthy ways of coping with life, and will model these to their children unless they break the codependency bonds.

Because codependent parents have a **desperate desire to be needed**, they may become overprotective of their children. They cannot let go because letting go would produce a void they cannot face. The children get the message that risk-taking and exploration are not okay because Mom or Dad makes them feel guilty if they take risks on their own.

When codependent parents suppress feelings, their children get the message that feelings are wrong. Games like "Let's Be Silent" and "Let's Pretend," result. Children of codependents, then, cannot express their feelings, either.

If codependent parents exhibit damaged self-esteem, they are unable to give or receive positive comments. So, children of codependents also develop damaged self-esteem because they usually only hear how things aren't okay.

I am fortunate that I had a few years to learn these things before Roger and I had children. When we moved back home and began to deal with Mom's chemical dependency, I tried to be very honest with my daughters, who were five, seven, and nine at that time. They knew Grandma had a disease long before chemical dependency became part of the school's curriculum. I also told them that they didn't have to accept responsibility for her problems because Grandma was sick even before they were born.

We don't have a perfect family by any means. But we do make a real effort to keep communication lines open. Family meal times continue to be sharing times even as the girls struggle through their teenage years (no TV during meals, not even for the Super Bowl). Even though we all keep busy schedules, we make it a point to save Sunday dinners for our family time so everyone can be together. We also manage to reserve an extra hour for talking time. We deal with things like calendars and lunch money, but we also deal with individual member needs and spiritual concerns.

My children know I love them. They know because I tell them. I hug them. I kiss them. Even though teenagers sometimes find it embarrassing to show affection, I know it builds their self-esteem to hear the words that someone cares about them.

I also try to be honest with them about my needs. When I need time to be alone, I ask for ten minutes of quiet (and we set a timer), and then I listen to their needs. When I feel lonely or sad and they ask about my mood, I reassure them they aren't the cause and tell them what is.

I try to practice the same openness and honesty with my other family members. My dad has now remarried. His wonderful wife, Barb, has helped him rebuild a positive relationship. As they added children, we became an extended family. With new sisters, Leslie and Laurie, and another brother, Luke, I've found that God has provided the missing elements of my earlier childhood in my "new" family. They understand, accept, and love me in a different way because they don't share in my chemical codependency. My "second" family provided a loving, normal, healthy relationship that helped me keep on track as I worked to shed my codependency bonds. I feel very blessed by them, indeed.

The way codependents relate in the family also extends to those outside the family. It's important to stomp out codependency bonds in every relationship.

Friends offer an enhancement to self-esteem that family members alone cannot provide. For one thing, friends usually see us more objectively. They aren't obligated to stay in a relationship, so when they do, it's because we matter to them. That makes us feel good.

Codependents often noticeably lack close friends. Unable to sustain close relationships because of their need to hide the chemically dependent person, codependents feel lonely. If they do form friendships, they usually seek out someone who needs them. Friends sustain their **desperate desire to be needed**. Friendships often become unhealthy or unbalanced as codependents impose a tighter and tighter grip on the relationship and eventually choke it to death. Most friends walk away when things become too restrictive, reinforcing the codependent's negative self-esteem.

Codependency can also spill over into working relationships. Unable to express needs or feelings, codependents take everything that happens personally and then they suppress it. When the boss doesn't say hello, for example, codependents often jump to the conclusion that they did something wrong because of their distorted perception of reality. Because codependents accept responsibility for their chemical dependents, they also accept responsibility for everything else that happens around them.

Codependents often find themselves passed over for promotions because they don't feel comfortable asking for better positions. Later on, they can't understand how it happened, and they don't connect their codependent behaviors to the loss.

Again, it is true that we are powerfully shaped by the events of the past. Patterns established in childhood will be repeated throughout life unless there is a conscious and deliberate effort to break them.

In order to grow, we have to give up some things and be willing to change. Jesus said, "He cuts off every branch in me that bears no fruit, while every branch that does bear fruit he trims so that it will be even more fruitful" (John 15:2).

Truly loving someone requires vulnerability. I loved my mother so much that I was willing to look at the log in my own eye. I was willing to risk sharing the truth, the reality of my life. And I was finally willing to break the bonds of codependency because I didn't want to stay where I was any longer.

The moment had come for the intervention—the opportunity to sit down together and communicate everything that had been happening to me in the process of preparing for this day. I thought these days, months, and even years of learning and coming to accept my role as a codependent were painful. I had no idea of the pain yet to come.

9

A "CARE"FRONTATION

I 'll probably never forget the day we sat down with Mom to "intervene" in her chemical dependency. It was a cold day in February. Outside, a snowstorm was furiously dumping a foot of snow on us.

I'll never know how I convinced Mom to meet with us. I had planned to take her for a ride in my new car and end up at the hospital, where the counseling team and my brothers were waiting. The snowstorm left me no choice but to be honest.

I remember pleading with Mom, telling her I needed to talk to her, that this was very important to me. I promised I would never again ask her to see a counselor if she would just hear me out this time. Secretly, I hoped it wouldn't be necessary. I couldn't tell her that my brothers would be there, or she'd have suspected something and never agreed to come.

We arrived an hour and a half late. I fervently prayed that the others hadn't given up. I couldn't risk calling them to explain our delay. They'd waited, thank goodness, but nerves were understandably tense.

Strangely enough, Mom didn't seem surprised to see my brothers. And when the counseling team introduced themselves, we all sat down. The chairs were arranged in a circle, probably to promote a feeling of closeness. To make us more comfortable, they offered coffee. Mom asked if she could smoke.

One of the counselors explained to Mom that we had some important feelings to share with her. They asked her to listen, without commenting, to everything we had to say. She would then have a chance to answer us. Mom agreed.

Mom's agreement to these conditions was an important step. From experience, the counselors knew that chemically dependent people often become defensive when confronted with the truth of their behavior. They try to sidetrack the issue by interrupting and flinging out accusations. The most effective way to reach them is to continually bombard them with facts until they are forced to see the truth.

And so we started. Everyone was so nervous. My youngest brother Richard spoke first, sharing his list and his feelings. He had to stop several times to regain control of his emotions.

My turn came next. I read from my prepared text:

Mom:

I came here today because I am deeply concerned about what's been happening to you. Your drinking seriously affects me *and* my family. What I have to say is painful, but I'd like to ask you to hear me out.

I don't think you realize how I feel when I see you drinking again. It takes me back to the times when I saw you drinking as a youngster. Very often, drinking made you unreasonable. For example, I needed your permission to sign up as a school guard in the sixth grade. When I came home, you were drinking. You flew into a rage and said "No!" You wanted me home. I felt so humiliated having to go back and say I couldn't do it. More embarrassing, I didn't have a reason why. I felt so angry—and afraid. I never knew how you would react to any request I made.

There were days when I wanted to invite my friends in or when I wanted to go out with them, but I couldn't. You constantly threw up after drinking, and I had to clean up the messes. I had to do most of the housework, too. I resented that. I felt cheated out of a normal life.

As your drinking got worse, most of the money we had went to buy bottles. When a bottle fell and I cut my knee badly, we couldn't afford a doctor, and I was so scared. I remember not telling anyone when I was hit by a car, either, because I was too afraid. I had hurt my arm, but you weren't able to get up and get help for me. When one of my teachers sent me to the nurse, she asked me why I hadn't seen a doctor. I felt too ashamed to admit you'd been drinking and couldn't take me, so I lied instead and said you were sick. I felt angry that I had to lie for you.

Finally, I became anxious and worried about what was happening to you. My schoolwork began to suffer. I cried a lot, but I refused to tell anyone at school why. I felt terrified that if they knew the truth, they'd take us away from you and you would die.

Then one day you stopped drinking. We never talked about how that happened. In many ways, it made such a difference in my life. You were able to do housekeeping chores again, and, for the first time, I felt free to develop friends and a life of my own. But because I felt a wall between us, I couldn't share my important feelings with you, and that hurt.

The years went by, and then something happened. Aunt Maybelle died four years ago. You appeared to take it well, but you refused to talk about your feelings. I had a need to talk, but you hung up, and that hurt me very much. Then things began to change. Your letters, which usually came twice a month, stopped coming. I'd enjoyed receiving them, and I felt shut out of your life. That hurt me, and I began to feel anxious about you.

We came to visit you in May of that year. When we went out for dinner, you ordered a drink with the rest of us. I felt a knot of fear in the pit of my stomach. I had not seen you take a drink since I was sixteen. I watched your behavior change from calm into giggly and weavy, and I wanted to throw up. I tried to pretend that there was nothing wrong.

Desperate to Be Needed

In the winter of 1978, you fell and broke your arm. I heard from Bruce and Richard that you'd been drinking again. Because I love you, I wanted to believe that you fell on the ice, sober, but I felt so distrustful and confused. I didn't know what to believe.

I tried calling to check on you, but I couldn't get an answer for three days. I felt so frantic that I called you at work. Your boss told me that you hadn't shown up for work, either. He had given you a warning slip because this wasn't the first time it had happened. I felt shocked.

As you may remember, we met with you shortly after that, now two years ago, to try and convince you to seek help. For the first time you shared your real feelings about some things. It wasn't easy, but we made a beginning. And I felt elated when you agreed to go with Richard to De Paul for counseling.

I felt so helpless when you then refused to go on with the program. But up to that point, I still hadn't seen you drinking, so I rationalized that things weren't so bad.

Then last summer I came to pick you up for your check-up. I had the girls with me, and we were going out to lunch. You wove down the stairs and refused to unlock the door and let us in. It was obvious to me that you had been drinking. When Amy asked, "What's the matter with Grandma, Mommy? She's acting funny," I felt so embarrassed and so angry. I wanted to slap you, and that horrified me. I loved you, but now you were hurting my family.

My inner frustration increased so that my physical health began to suffer. Outbreaks of skin allergies became so violent that I could no longer cope. I knew that somehow this situation had to be resolved. So, Roger found a job and we moved up north.

Just after we arrived, you had another fall—this time breaking your back and your foot. I knew you had been drinking and had blacked out. When I came in and saw the bloodstains on the floor a week later, I felt sick to my stomach—and I hurt inside, thinking how much worse it could have been. When I went upstairs, you were throwing up, and I felt so sorry for you—and angry with myself. It was as if the clock had rolled back and nothing had ever changed.

74

A *"Care"frontation*

A few weeks later, I decided to see a counselor. I dropped by to ask you to go with me. I surprised you just coming home from the grocery. We sat down in the living room and talked about everyday things, while inside I felt like screaming. Suddenly I took a closer look at you and saw that you were sitting on a bottle. A moment later, I noticed another one in a bag next to the couch. I could have cried! You looked so pathetic sitting on that bottle, and I felt so helpless trying to talk to you.

Going downtown in December, I finally realized how much your health had been affected by your drinking. You could barely walk, you were winded, and you couldn't climb up the curb without help. I didn't think you would make the two blocks we had to walk. I suddenly saw you as a really old person, and I felt so sorry for you.

And now you've lost your job. Your boss called me to explain. He revealed that on four separate occasions this year, you had to be taken home because you had been drinking and couldn't perform your duties as a nurse. I felt so ashamed.

Mom, when you drink you become a different person. I am frightened by your mood changes. You laugh at things that aren't funny, you repeat yourself, and then you get angry with me. A day or two later, you can't even remember that I called.

On the other hand, there's such a difference when you're sober. I really enjoyed going downtown with you and the girls for breakfast. My girls were so happy to share a treat with Grandma. And what a joyful feeling to attend church on Christmas Eve together as a family. Having you with us on Christmas, sober, turned it into a special occasion. Alcohol does make a difference.

Other people notice the difference, too. Your boss made a point of telling me that you'd be missed at work. He told me that he wrote on your report that he would recommend rehiring you *if* you would enroll in a rehabilitation program. He thinks there's hope for you.

I think there's hope for you, too. Because I love you, I'm asking you to get help today, before it's too late.

I barely made it through the recitation. Once again, the boxes of Kleenex came in handy.

My other brother Bruce then shared his list. He appeared to be the calmest, although his voice betrayed his feelings. He read quietly and ended with the same appeal the rest of us had used.

The counselors summarized by outlining to Mom the kind of help we were suggesting. They briefly explained the rehabilitation program and what it could do for her. Then they asked for Mom's response.

We hadn't been able to judge much from her expressions as we talked. She refused to take off her coat and looked as if she might fly out of the room at any moment. Once she smoked a cigarette. Occasionally, she brushed away a tear. Nothing in her face gave us a clue about what she felt as we honestly shared with her what we saw happening. When finally given a chance to speak, she simply said, "No."

I had expected a rebuttal, arguments, defensive statements, accusations. Anything but this cold and chilling "No." Now what were we going to do?

The counselors had anticipated this reaction and had instructed us to prepare a "clout" statement. We had one more opportunity to get our point across.

Quickly they explained to Mom that because of her answer, we had some other important feelings to share with her. We knew it would be our last chance to convince her.

My brothers simply stated that if Mom refused help, they wanted nothing more to do with her. They were tired of their codependency bonds, and they wanted to break them. They were more than happy to work with her through a rehabilitation program if Mom agreed to get help. Either Mom wanted a productive life again, or she wanted the bottle. She couldn't have both.

My voice was choked as I read:

Mom:

You know that I have a tremendous faith in God. From the very beginning, I've believed that somehow the problem with your drinking was going to work out. I encouraged my brothers to hang on through these darkest hours because I believed that we could get through to you.

My human nature turned many of the feelings I had to anger and hatred. I felt I had the right to those feelings. It wasn't until I met God and came to know his forgiving love that I could begin to understand what love really is. Sometimes that means putting on God's eyeglasses and looking through the outside person to see what's inside the heart.

The reason I could offer encouragement to my brothers through all this is because I looked at you with God's glasses and saw inside to the person God created you to be. I know that underneath your hard exterior lies a kernel of beauty. With the proper help and much understanding, that kernel can grow into the beautiful person God designed you to be.

It will break my heart if you refuse help today. But I also know that loving someone means letting go of them. I never thought that I would reach the point of letting you go. As I prayed in recent weeks and asked God to help me know what to do, his answer was this: God gives every person a choice. Now you must choose. If you refuse help today, you are as good as dead. Physically, you cannot keep drinking without killing yourself. And if you don't get help today, I'm walking out this door, and I'll have nothing more to do with you.

As much as it would hurt me to walk out of your life, it would kill me to stand by and watch you die.

I moved up here with my family to work together with you and my brothers to build the family God wants us to be. I desperately want to have you with us. There is only one thing that stands between us—and that one thing is a bottle. You have to make a choice as to what's most important to you—the bottle or your family. I'm hoping you'll choose us.

The tears were streaming down my face. I looked once more at my mother's face, silently pleading with her to listen to me. She looked at us and softly repeated, "No."

I felt a great anger welling up inside and was grateful for the counseling team. At that moment, they asked us to sit quietly for a few minutes and think through what had been said.

After a moment or two, I became aware that everyone in the room was watching for my reactions. Through the last four years, I had felt so positive that God would grant my request and that I would see my mother cured. Whenever my brothers doubted, I supplied them with Scriptures for encouragement. My God wouldn't fail—yet apparently he had.

I reflected on the hell that the past four years had been. I thought about all the pain we'd endured, and the humiliation, and the embarrassment. I had managed to hold on through it all, because I earnestly believed that in the end we would succeed.

Now, I had to face living up to the brave words I'd spoken. I told Mom I'd walk out and never see her again. I believed it was the right thing to do. Silently I pleaded with God to send me a word of encouragement, something to sustain me, for I needed him now more than ever.

Suddenly the Scripture from Luke 22:31 sprang into my mind. I had read it earlier that morning. "Janet, Janet, behold Satan demanded to have you, that he might sift you like wheat, but I have prayed for you, that your faith might not fail" (RSV).

The thought was electrifying. Was *my* faith being tested here? How *was* I going to react to my mother's decision? Would I obey God, and walk out as I felt he was telling me to do? Or would I fall into Satan's trap?

God knew what he was doing. He had built a foundation of faithfulness in me all these years. I'd never had a reason to doubt him before, and I didn't have one now. I felt the comfort of his loving arms surround me in that room, and I knew that everything would somehow be okay. Even though I couldn't understand right now, someday I would. It was enough for me to know that God was still in charge.

Everyone waited for me to denounce God, to get angry, but I couldn't. I had nothing more to say. It really was over. Mom had made her choice, and I couldn't blame God, even though I felt terribly torn apart.

It took everything I had to get up, take my coat, and walk out of the room, believing I would never see my mother again. We had lost, and now I had to accept that fact and go about the business of putting the pieces of my life together again. Even though Mom had refused help, I knew *I* was ready for recovery. I was ready to be healed, thanks to the knowledge and wisdom God had brought to me about my role as a codependent.

10

RECOVERY: HEALING
THE REAL HURTS

T o this point, I've described how to recognize chemical dependency, and I've defined codependency as a **desperate desire to be needed**, so desperate that the codependent will sacrifice personal needs to the illness.

I've described some of the roles spouses and children play in a codependent family. I've pointed out how family, friends, and coworkers serve as enablers, allowing the chemical dependency to continue.

All of these are part of **Step 1** in recovery: recognizing the need for help. I personally believe that this is the hardest step to take.

Tearing down the denial defense system leaves the codependent standing exposed. So, I've talked about the feelings surrounding recognition of codependency, the damaged self-esteem that results from codependency, the effects of codependency on various relationships, and the programs available for help.

Step 2 in recovery involves identifying the facts and feelings in codependency and assessing the impact on one's life. Step 2 involves accepting responsibility for those facts

Desperate to Be Needed

and feelings by expressing them in "I" messages to the chemically dependent person.

Naturally, then, **Step 3** in recovery leads to some kind of intervention. Because the codependent genuinely cares about the chemically dependent person, there is the desire that confrontation be a "care"frontation. Step 3 challenges the codependent to express that care honestly, with the objective of bringing the chemically dependent person to a recognition of the reality the codependent has already faced.

But what happens if the chemically dependent person fails to respond to the codependent's plea? The answer to this question moves us to a critical **fourth step** in recovery: the need for accepting that we are not responsible for the chemically dependent's decision.

After failing, it would be very easy at this point to move back into the codependent role. Codependents could now spend all of their time trying to understand why the chemically dependent person refused help. It's very tempting to circle back into blame (If only my brother had been more emphatic), self-doubt (Do I have the right to interfere in her life?), and damaged self-esteem (She never really loved me or she would have said yes).

After we left Mom, I lapsed into that kind of negative thinking. I felt so angry and bitter and hurt. I couldn't understand how God could have allowed this to happen. And I still felt responsible.

"God does not hold us responsible for results, but He does hold us responsible for what we do and how we do it," writes James Pittman of Radio Bible Ministries.[1] Part of breaking the codependency chain meant accepting that I wasn't responsible for Mom's decision. Neither was God. I was only responsible for confronting her and doing it as lovingly as Jesus would have done.

Did I love my mother? Absolutely! I doubt that many would have gone to the lengths I went to help her. Wasn't that proof of my love? What more could I have done?

As I thought and prayed about what to do next, I had to ask myself the questions again: Do I truly love my mother? If so, how can I walk away and leave her? What will happen to her now? What will other people think?

I didn't realize it at the time, but I was walking the thin line of codependency again. Removing the object of my desperate need left me with a huge void. And once again, I was looking at the log in Mom's eye and avoiding the one in my own.

What do you do with a broken relationship? Give it to Jesus to mend. I had to trust him enough to put Mom in his hands and let go. Could I do that as a codependent?

At this point, I must admit I felt hatred for my mother. Why couldn't she see what she was doing? Why would she choose to walk away from her family? Didn't she know how much we cared?

I found I was still looking at the wrong person. I didn't see that *I* had the problem, not Mom. I felt no peace, and in desperation I kept pounding the doors of heaven for answers.

I felt a little exasperated, like Simon Peter must have felt when Jesus asked him three times, "Do you love me?" Each time, Peter answered, "You know I do." And Jesus responded, "Feed My sheep," or "Tend my flock." Why three times? Wasn't once enough? I think Jesus wanted Peter to take his focus off the one he loved (Jesus) and place it on those who were left behind and in need of a leader.

God was telling me that my love for Mom wasn't in question. However, it was time for me to step aside and get back to the business he had for me: to break the bonds of codependency, once and for all.

I now had to make a choice. I could continue to behave as a codependent, or I could give it up. How did I do that?

Step 5 in recovery involves looking at the circumstances, the hurt feelings, the emotions, and the damaged self-esteem, and putting them under God's spotlight of forgiveness. This involves learning to forgive, and then to forget, so that the codependent can truly be free.

What does it mean to consciously forgive someone? Dr. James Dobson, in describing tough love, cautions people against developing resentment. "It can be a malignancy that consumes the spirit and warps the mind, leaving us bitter and disappointed with life. I'll say it again: no matter how badly we've been mistreated or how selfish our partners have seemed, we are called upon to release them from accountability. That is the meaning of forgiveness. According to psychologist Archibald Hart, "Forgiveness is surrendering my *right* to hurt you for hurting me."[2]

Dr. Robert Schuller offered a slightly different answer in counseling someone who hurts. "Forgiveness doesn't mean you have to approve his behavior! You could never do that! But forgiveness does mean you are going to put it behind you—and yes, in practical terms, forget it! Which means you'll bury the hatchet and not leave the handle above the ground! But to forgive and forget does not mean you have to have a restored relationship! You don't even need to become friends. You just have to stop being enemies!"[3]

A person still locked in the bonds of codependency tries to ignore the hurt and pain and hopes it will go away. A codependent believes the relationship has to be restored because of that **desperate desire to be needed**. A person still locked in codependency blames someone else for the problems.

A healthy person recognizes the hurt and pain and accepts the fact that these things have happened. A healthy person can let go. A healthy person will put the experience behind, by forgiving and forgetting.

I wanted to be healthy and whole, not codependent. How could I forgive and forget? With God's help, I began what some people call a healing of memories.

Step by step, I went through the incidents on my list. As Dr. Glasser would say, I set about to change the pictures in my memory album. Instead of seeing these events as crippling, I would put a new framework around them.

For each picture, I said, "Mom didn't deliberately try to hurt me. Mom was sick, and she couldn't cope with her problems, so she _____." I then pictured Mom as Jesus saw her—whole, well, doing the things a real mom would have done in this situation. That's what Mom really wanted to do. Then, in my mind's eye, I clicked the camera, and I had a new picture to replace the old one.

Robert Subby and John Friel call it getting in touch with the child within. "At birth, our private and public self are equal. As we learn to deny, our real self gets stuck and our public self gets distorted. To change, we need to make friends with and nurture the child within us whom we left behind."[4]

Replacing those pictures wasn't easy. It took time. I had a lot of attitudes to change.

Albert Ellis, noted psychologist from the Institute of Rational Living in New York, lists ten common *self-defeating* attitudes which cause unnecessary pain and frustration.[5] Although I don't necessarily agree with all he's written, I did find Scripture verses that give the biblical view and have listed them alongside each negative attitude. I call these the ten steps to a healthier codependent.

1. "The idea that you must—yes, must—have love or approval from all the people you find significant."

Brother will betray brother to death, and a father his child. Children will rebel against their parents and have them put to death. All men will hate you because of me, but he who stands firm to the end will be saved (Mark 13:12–13).

2. "The idea that you must prove thoroughly competent, adequate, and achieving; or a saner but still foolish variation: The idea that you must have competence or talent in some important area."

If I must boast, I will boast of the things that show my weakness (2 Cor. 11:30).

3. "The idea that when people act obnoxiously and unfairly, you should blame and damn them, and see them as bad, wicked, or rotten individuals."

"If any one of you is without sin, let him be the first to throw a stone at her .... Has no one condemned you? ... Then neither do I condemn you" (John 8:7–11).

4. "The idea that you have to view things as awful, terrible, horrible, and catastrophic when you get seriously frustrated, treated unfairly, or rejected."

I have learned to be content whatever the circumstances (Phil. 4:11).

5. "The idea that emotional misery comes from external pressures and that you have little ability to control or change your feelings."

Choose for yourselves this day whom you will serve (Josh. 24:15).

6. "The idea that if something seems dangerous or fearsome, you must preoccupy yourself with and make yourself anxious about it."

Therefore do not be anxious about tomorrow, for tomorrow will be anxious for itself (Matt. 6:34 RSV).

7. "The idea that you can more easily avoid facing many of life's difficulties and self-responsibilities than undertake more rewarding forms of self-discipline."

Therefore keep watch, because you do not know the day or the hour (Matt. 25:13).

8. "The idea that your past remains all important and that because something once influenced your life, it has to keep determining your feelings and behavior today."

Therefore, if anyone is in Christ, he is a new creation; the old has passed away, behold, the new has come (2 Cor. 5:17 RSV).

9. "The idea that people and things should turn out better than they do and that you must view it as awful and terrible if you do not find good solutions to life's grim realities."

Consider it pure joy, my brothers, whenever you face trials of many kinds (James 1:2).

10. "The idea that you can achieve maximum human happiness by inertia and inaction or by passively and uncommittedly "enjoying yourself."

Fear not, little flock, for it is your Father's good pleasure to give you the kingdom. Sell your possessions, and give alms; provide yourselves with purses that do not grow old, with a treasure in the heavens that does not fail, where no thief approaches and no moth destroys. For where your treasure is, there will your heart be also (Luke 12:32–34 RSV).

When I finished letting go of the self-defeating attitudes, I was ready for God to teach me the lesson he wanted me to learn: "Therefore we do not lose heart. Though outwardly we are wasting away, yet inwardly we are being renewed day by day. For our light and momentary troubles are achieving for us an eternal glory that far outweighs them all. So we fix our eyes not on what is seen, but on what is unseen. For what is seen is temporary, but what is unseen is eternal" (2 Cor. 4:16–18).

God is the only one who knows what lies ahead. As I thought about my "momentary defeat," I realized he was asking me if I would be willing to trust him for my future.

Then I read Romans 8:35, 37: "Who shall separate us from the love of Christ? Shall trouble or hardship or persecution or famine or nakedness or danger or sword? . . . . No, in all these things we are more than conquerors through him who loved us." Translation: Would this disappointment, this experience destroy me, or would I choose to overcome it?

At last, I gave my answer. I visualized letting go of Mom's hand and putting her in his care, and I experienced God's peace for the first time in my life.

Though I began to accept what happened, I still had a need to know why things ended this way. I prayed, I prepared, I spoke in love, and I failed. Was *I* guilty of some unknown sin that God decided needed punishment?

As if to reassure me once more, God brought to my attention an interesting account in Luke 16:19–31. In this story, a rich man and a poor man died on the same day. The poor man went to heaven, and the rich man went off to hell. Looking up from hell, the rich man called for the poor man to give him some water, but his request was refused. So the rich man asked that the poor man be sent to his house to warn his brothers, so that they might repent in time. Abraham replied, "If they do not listen to Moses and the Prophets, they will not be convinced even if someone rises from the dead" (v. 31).

Now the Lord asked me, "Who had the choice to make— you or your mother?"

"Mother," I answered.

"And what did you pray for?" he asked.

"I prayed that she might hear what we said and choose you, God."

"Did she hear what you said?"

"Yes."

"Then your prayers were answered. Satan was bound and your mother heard you. She made a choice, one that we both feel badly about, but the choice was hers to make, not yours. It would have made no difference if the circumstances had been different, or if your words were different, or if you had changed the day, or anything. As this verse says, even sending someone from the dead wouldn't have helped. Your mother hardened her heart by her own choice. Let go of her now and relinquish her care to me."

What a beautiful moment of release I experienced then! I realized the truth of what I'd just read and heard. No matter how much I wanted my mother to be helped, she had to want that for herself.

I felt comforted, realizing that God shared the same frustration I felt. No matter how much he wants us to follow his way, he won't force himself upon us if we refuse. He leaves the choice up to us.

I also recognized that I had been plagued by doubts for these past few weeks, doubts that I could not confess as sin. I was ready for the last step of recovery.

Dr. Bernard Siegel wrote, "Finding the ability to love requires giving up the fear, anguish, and despair that many people nurture. Many people have a lifetime of unresolved anger circulating through their minds and causing new stress with each recall. Confronting them and letting go of them involves honestly facing your own part in the problem, and forgiving yourself as well as the others you've resented and feared. If you do not forgive, you become like your enemy."[6]

If you do not forgive, you remain a codependent. I didn't want to be a codependent any more. So, I went through my mental picture album one more time, and where I had condemned myself, I confessed my sin and asked for forgiveness. I then replaced each picture with a new one showing the joy I felt at being forgiven.

Just as chemical dependents do not live in isolation, neither do codependents. In order to experience full recovery, **Step 6** requires restoring relationships with new guidelines. After first deciding what unhealthy behaviors I wanted to give up, I had to take the time to ask others for forgiveness and explain how I hoped to change my codependent behaviors.

The **last step** in breaking codependency calls for seeking a balance between the needs of the codependent and the needs of others. Either extreme is harmful. I no longer had a **desperate desire to be needed**, but I still wanted to be needed. My goals would be to find ways to satisfy both my needs and those of others who mattered to me.

I also had a need to write out my experiences. I wrote *Beloved Alcoholic,* published by Zondervan in 1984 (and now out of print). Writing helped me put things into perspective, but I also wanted others to know it was okay to fail. Then it happened. Just before the book came off the press, I received the call that would eventually lead to the words I had longed to hear: "Please help me." I didn't know it then, but I would still face more difficult choices, each more difficult than the previous one.

11

CHOICES

The first call was from my aunt, Mom's sister. Mom had called her to report the sheriff was coming to evict her, and Mom needed help. My aunt asked if I would go.

I knew my aunt had no idea what a difficult thing she was asking. I had spent years breaking the codependency chains and, just when I felt I'd conquered them, I was being challenged again. In just one call, I faced the possibility of walking right back into the same bondage. Was I strong enough? Was I ready? What did God want me to do?

I shut myself up with my Bible that afternoon to seek God's answer. I shivered when I read James 2:15–16: "Suppose a brother or sister is without clothes and daily food. If one of you says to him, 'Go, I wish you well; keep warm and well fed,' but does nothing about his physical needs, what good is it?"

I believed God was sending me a clear message. I could offer Mom the necessities of life, along with my help, but I would not become a codependent again. I had to be very clear with me and then with Mom about what I was willing to do.

I went on to read these verses from Luke 14:27–28: "And

anyone who does not carry his cross and follow me cannot be my disciple. Suppose one of you wants to build a tower. Will he not first sit down and estimate the cost to see if he has enough money to complete it?"

God was right. I needed to count the cost and decide if I was willing to pay it.

"Ask of me, and I will make the nations your inheritance, the ends of the earth your possession" (Psalm 2:8). I needed God's help if I was going to claim the victory for Mom and for myself, the codependent. God reassured me that the end result was all that mattered: possessing a whole family.

Then I read these words and again my spine tingled: "Now finish the work, so that your eager willingness to do it may be matched by your completion of it, according to your means" (2 Cor. 8:11).

Oh, dear God, I thought. *Are you telling me I have what it takes to do this thing?* I received a clear message, spelled out for me so that I would have no doubts. I knew then what I had to do. Trembling, I picked up the phone and called Mom.

It was funny, but God had helped me maintain contact with her though I hadn't actually seen her for the past three years. The first summer I'd received a phone call from a cousin I hadn't seen in twenty years. He suddenly decided to drop by and visit Mom. Wondering if she was sick because she didn't look well, he called me to find out. I never heard from him again. I knew his call wasn't a coincidence. God wanted to reassure me that all was well.

I'd received two other calls, though, from strangers who had spoken to Mom and called me to report. I don't know how they got my number. I only know that they carried a comforting message. God was continuing to watch over Mom.

When Mom answered the phone, my heart stopped. Could it really be possible that after three years she was ready for help?

I told her why I was calling, and I offered to help her in this way: I would come and help her pack up her things and take them to a storage area—nothing more. We would have to talk later about where to go from there.

The next two days would press our Christian faith to the maximum as my husband and I drove down to help Mom pack. Nothing had prepared us for the conditions in which Mom lived. I saw what the pit of degradation looked like, and it was awful. I don't know how Roger and I stuck it out, except that God gave us extraordinary strength.

My mother, sixty years old then, looked like a woman of eighty. She could not walk through the apartment without limping, and her breathing sounded terrible.

The apartment was filthy, with cockroaches crawling over everything, including Mom herself. Her hair was so matted to her head that I almost had to shave it off. And she smelled. I remember thinking, *Dear God, how could anyone live like this?*

We packed all through the night. The sheriff arrived early the next morning. Because he saw our attempts to get Mom moved, he compromised and gave us another twenty-four hours. "However . . . ." the sheriff warned, "your mother has had several notices already . . . ." I knew the rest and was just grateful for the reprieve.

The next day, when my brothers found out what I was doing, they were angry with me. They feared I was still playing the family hero, enabling Mom to avoid the consequences of her actions one more time.

I knew they were being honest with me. It wouldn't take much to become a codependent again. I made it very clear to them that I would do nothing more than pack her things, and that's all we did. We found a storage unit nearby, rented a truck, and by the end of day two we'd moved everything over.

Now came the difficult moment of decision. What did Mom want to do? I offered her two choices. She could come back with us, but only if she signed in for treatment. Otherwise, we'd drop her off downtown and she could figure out how to live with her chemical dependency. At that moment, it really didn't matter to me what she decided to do.

After a long period of silence, Mom said, "I want help." Those were the most beautiful words! I know the bells of heaven rang out! At last, we were going to move ahead into the healed whole family I always dreamed of having.

Now I needed more information about "aftercare." From previous research, I knew that aftercare is "that period of time that provides a bridge from the initial treatment experience to the goal of a healthier family system. It offers the chemical dependent and the loved ones the time and opportunity to find effective solutions to use when the old problems return."[1]

After all, we'd learned some very negative ways of interacting with each other. Now, Mom and I needed to find new ground—one that would allow me to remain free of codependency and yet help her meet needs, too.

I found out that our local hospital could only provide a short stay to help Mom "dry out." They had an outpatient program, however, in which Mom could participate for two years. And there was a full treatment facility about fifty miles away. Though the distance would make aftercare more difficult, I wanted to support Mom in any way I could, even if it meant driving that far every week.

I drove Mom to see her sister, and together we discussed Mom's need for help. I knew it was important to offer my mother some choices, so I explained the different program options. Mom chose the short-term hospital visit with the outpatient arrangement. She would stay with my family until she was ready to be on her own. I was so proud of my family. The girls agreed to give up a bedroom so Grandma could have her own room. They gave Mom such positive reinforcement. We'd worked hard on being open and honest with each other, and now Mom had a chance to see up close how well things could work out.

Twice a week I took Mom to see the local rehabilitation

counselors. One day she met with a group, and the other day she met individually with the counselor. It wasn't easy for her because the group members were all younger and had very different problems from hers, but I admired Mom for trying.

Mom really made the effort to get her life on track. Her sister started dropping by for visits. And Mom began filling out because she was eating regularly and taking care of herself.

The only hitch in my happiness came when my youngest brother, Richard, refused to believe that things were going so well, although I invited him to see for himself. I finally got tired of his shouting and fussing at me and told him either to come up and talk to us or leave us alone. I had enough to deal with, and his anger wasn't helping. I didn't know then that he himself suffered from a chemical dependency.

My other brother, Bruce, had moved to Arizona with his family, seeking a new life away from the reminders of the past. He also called and asked questions—out of concern, not condemnation. I know it was hard being so far away; I'd experienced the same feelings when I was living in Florida.

We finally found Mom an apartment about six blocks from us. In the interest of an open and honest relationship, I asked her to read my book, *Beloved Alcoholic*, before she left. She didn't like the book; it made her feel uncomfortable. She did agree, though, that I was entitled to my perspective of what happened, and we left it at that.

As Mom continued in therapy, I joined an Al-Anon group. I needed the support of others who had walked this ground before me. Most of them, however, were dealing with people who were still drinking. I felt fortunate that I had that behind me.

I was also grateful to our pastor and his wife. Their love and acceptance of my mother paved the way for others. Our church really reached out to make Mom feel welcome. It was doubly important to Mom because she knew that everyone had heard all about her, and yet loved and accepted her anyway.

When Mom moved into her own place, I believed we were well on the way to making it. Mom could be independent, yet we were close enough to help if needed. And Mom could participate in the grandchildren's activities. That first year, she didn't miss a concert, a school affair, or an awards program—she took as much pride in their accomplishments as we did.

I think we would have made it, too. And then . . . there was another phone call bringing us bad news . . . and another challenge to our faith.

The person calling was a friend of my youngest brother. Richard had been rushed to a hospital in a coma. The friend finally confessed that my brother had accidentally mixed drugs and alcohol. When they found him, he wasn't breathing. I called the emergency room and learned that the doctors had restored his breathing, but they couldn't predict whether or not he would come out of the coma. They advised us to drive down as quickly as we could.

I can only remember thinking that day of a song phrase as we drove the two hours to the hospital. "Quiet, please, too much has already been said. Let it be, and learn to listen instead."[2] That phrase would somehow sustain me through the tragic events of the following days.

The doctors tried valiantly to save my brother's life, but it was too late. He never regained consciousness. And we never had a chance to say the things that were in our hearts. "Quiet, please, too much has already been said. Let it be, and learn to listen instead."

It still hurts to talk about Richard's death. What is the price of chemical dependency? Sometimes it is life itself. Standing at his grave, I felt so sad. Yet I knew my other brother and I were in danger of becoming codependents again unless we acted swiftly to get help.

Mom explained to everyone in town that her son had died

in the service. I wanted to confront her and make her face the truth, but her counselors cautioned me that I might push Mom over the edge if I forced the issue.

As the day of the funeral approached, though, I knew I needed to express some of my feelings to Mom. I asked our pastor's wife, Liz, to go with me so that the conversation wouldn't get bogged down by heavy emotions. I also appreciated her prayer support.

Though my mother and dad hadn't seen each other in years, I wanted my father to come to the funeral. I knew Dad loved Richard. It was critical that they bury the twenty-seven years of hatred and experience forgiveness so Mom could move on with the healing in her life.

I told Mom how God had forgiven me and how I'd learned to forgive her, too. I quoted Dr. Schuller's comment that forgiving doesn't mean having a restored relationship; it just means that you stop being enemies. I asked Mom to bury her hatred with Richard and allow Dad to share in the loss of their son.

Mom promised to think about it. I think she was surprised by my honesty. And I know I was surprised and touched when Mom approached Dad at the end of the funeral service and shook his hand.

I suppose I shouldn't have been surprised when, four months later, Roger saw Mom buying beer. I did not confront her. This time, Mom was honest with me. "Isn't everyone entitled to make a mistake?" she asked. Things *had* been rough, and I could understand that. It had been rough for all of us. But I felt confident that having beaten chemical dependency twice, we could beat it a third time. I should have known . . . .

12

THE END IS
JUST THE BEGINNING

Nothing quite prepares you for the end when it comes. Once again, the phone rang. This time, the caller was telling us that my mother had been found dead in her apartment. Apparently she had had a heart attack after coming out of the shower the night before.

At long last, this chapter of my life was closing, whether I was ready or not. Once again, I pounded the doors of heaven with questions and tears.

I shall never forget the memorial service Pastor Karl conducted. He centered his comments around one question he had repeatedly asked Mom: "What am I going to say about you?" What could anyone say about Mom?

Pastor Karl recognized the beauty Mom held inside her. He'd seen her sense of humor, her giving nature, her inquisitive mind. They'd spent many hours debating Scriptural issues. Mom had been a beautiful, intelligent woman before she became chemically dependent.

Pastor Karl also knew Mom's dark side. He'd never seen Mom out of control, but he had seen others. He knew—so what could he say?

Once when we traveled out west, I saw a famous statue

called "The End of the Trail" at the National Cowboy Museum. The statue depicts a once-proud Indian warrior bent over his trusted horse, who also looks dejected and ready to give up. The magnificent sculpture is quietly eloquent. It shows the pain of the sad end to a once-proud people.

That's how I felt when we buried my mother. We had reached the end of the trail. It was a sad end to a once-proud person. I had to accept that this world no longer held heartache for my mother. She rested in peace at last.

When I went through her papers a few days later, I discovered some shocking facts. Mom had gone back to serious drinking, to the tune of five-hundred dollars a month. I don't know how she got the alcohol, but it was obvious she'd been drinking that much because she'd saved the receipts. It was almost as if she had wanted to be caught.

I'd had no idea. Oh, once or twice I'd catch a whiff of alcohol, or her behavior would seem unusual, but I chalked it up to my imagination, or to the smell that permeated her clothing. When I realized later to what lengths she had gone to hide her condition, I wondered if I had just refused to see it.

Why did my mother lapse into chemical dependency a third time? A conversation during one of our last outings best answers that question. Mom's birthday often fell on or near Mother's Day. This last year of her life, the dates happened to coincide. As a treat, we'd taken her out to a fancy restaurant for lunch. I'd also arranged for a perm the week before, so Mom looked extra-special, and the girls had presented her with a corsage at the table.

Back at home, over cake and coffee, we gave her an electric broom. She loved it, as she'd been complaining that her back hurt from pushing her old Kirby. On the way home, however, Mom insisted on writing out a check to pay for part of the vacuum. "It was too much," she protested, and she wouldn't take no for an answer. I remember turning and gazing at her in astonishment, even though I was driving. Then I said, "But Mom, don't you know you're worth it? I think you are!"

Mom never believed she was "worth it." She never accepted that she deserved more. This world just didn't offer her the peace she so desperately sought. Who was I to question God if dying brought her peace at last?

Once again, I had to make a choice. Would I lock myself into codependency again? Was I truly free now, too? I could choose to be bitter or better, as Dr. Schuller would say. Would I hate Mom for hurting me one more time, or would I forgive her yet again?

I chose to leave the happy picture I had of Mom's last years in my memory album. It would serve no purpose to fill my album with anger or bitterness or hate. Mom's chemical dependency was *her* problem. I chose not to make it mine.

One of my friends shared a poem with me to help me put Mom's death into perspective:

> Death is truly a door to more instead of less,
> A plus instead of a minus,
> An increase instead of a decrease,
> A gift instead of a travesty,
> A filling instead of an emptying,
> An eternal instead of a finite,
> A birthday instead of a wake!
> So, Happy Birthday.[1]

Once again, I sat down to write out my experiences. For me, writing is a good way to sort out everything that has happened and put it into perspective. And just as I put my notes together for this manuscript, I received one more call that brought news of yet another change in my life.

After four years, my dad has finally sold the lake cottage our family owned since before I was born. It was the only home I knew, my refuge from life's storms, and now it, too, would be gone. I thought it was fitting that I should go there for the last time to finish writing these last two chapters.

There are so many happy pictures of this place in my memory album. Today, I took my last walk down the road that winds around the island. It's hard to believe that we won't be back here again next spring.

And yet, as I walk and clear my head and get in touch with nature, I hear God speaking to me. Yes, we've had some good times in this cottage, but it's just a house, a temporary shelter. There will be other times, other places. The house itself is not really that important.

Why is this such a happy place? I guess it's because I've enjoyed the people, my family and friends, the relationships we've built here, the good conversations long into the night around the dining room table.

People and relationships are transient. As much as we'd like to keep them near us always, there comes a time when we have to learn to let them go, too.

As God continues to talk to me while I walk, I realize that the bonds of codependency truly have been broken. As a codependent, I wouldn't have been able to endure leaving this place. I would have feared letting go. I would have fought to keep it.

Now I know that the only permanent thing I have in life is my faith, not places or people. Faith gives meaning to my existence. God gives me a purpose for living.

As I close the cottage door for the last time, I symbolically close the door on this chapter of my life. I am a sojourner here on earth, a temporary resident, and it's time to move on. As I look up, I see the road, the road that ends at the cottage door, the end of the trail.

But God reminds me that the end of the road is also its beginning. The road leads me on to yet another place. Though one part of my life has ended, another part has just begun.

I get behind the wheel of my car and realize, that like life, I'm in the driver's seat. I choose the road that I'll take, and I choose the passengers who will ride with me. I'm in charge, not somebody else. I'm glad God created me that way!

I pull out, unafraid of what lies ahead. I know God's there to guide me, to point me in the right direction, to show me how to get repairs if I break down along the way. I have only to ask.

God created me to be loving. He taught me how to love my mother, as difficult as that was at times. As Dr. Schuller wrote, "Although love can hurt, although love can bring disappointment, pain and rejection—*real* love also brings with it possibilities!"[2]

As Amanda McBroom says so beautifully in her song, "The Rose":

Some say love, it is a river that drowns the tender reed.
Some say love, it is a razor that leaves your heart to bleed.
Some say love, it is a hunger, an endless, aching need;
I say love it is a flower, and you its only seed.

It's the heart afraid of breaking, that never learns to dance.
It's the dream afraid of waking, that never takes a chance.
It's the one who won't be taken, who cannot seem to give;
And the soul afraid of dying, that never learns to live.

When the night has been too lonely,
And the road has been too long,
And you think that love is only for the lucky and the strong,
Just remember, in the winter, far beneath the bitter snows,
Lies the seed that with the sun's love,
In the spring, becomes the rose.*

As a codependent, I needed to fill my **desperate desire to be needed**. I wouldn't take chances for fear of losing control. I never learned to live.

Because of the Son's love, I have learned to love, first myself and then the others around me. I know now, wherever

---

my journey takes me from here, that God goes with me, and I am free of codependency at last!

"For he is our peace, who has made us both one, and has broken down the dividing wall of hostility . . . So then you are no longer strangers and sojourners, but you are fellow citizens with the saints and members of the household of God" (Eph. 2:14, 19 RSV).

"For I know the plans I have for you," declares the LORD, "plans to prosper you and not to harm you, plans to give you hope and a future. Then you will call upon me and come and pray to me, and I will listen to you. You will seek me and find me when you seek me with all your heart. I will be found by you," declares the LORD, "and will bring you back from captivity. I will gather you from all the nations and places where I have banished you," declares the LORD, "and will bring you back to the place from which I carried you into exile" (Jer. 29:11–14).

"But who am I, and what is my people, that we should be able thus to offer willingly? For all things come from thee, and of thy own have we given thee. For we are strangers before thee, and sojourners, as all our fathers were; our days on the earth are like a shadow, and there is no abiding" (1 Chron. 29:14–15 RSV).

May God bless your journey! Thanks for walking a while with me as I travel mine!

ENDNOTES

Chapter 1

[1] Thomas R. McCabe, *Victims No More* (Center City, Minn.: Hazelden Educational Materials, 1978), 10.

[2] Kay Bartlett, "Alcoholism: Drink Debate," *Green Bay Press Gazette* (March 24, 1985).

[3] Michael D'Antonion, "Unsafe At Every Speed," *Family Weekly* (December 26, 1982), 25.

[4] Dr. Robert Anthony, *The Ultimate Secrets of Total Self-Confidence* (New York: Berkley Books, 1979), 1–2.

Chapter 2

[1] Dr. Alan Levin and Merla Zellerback, *Type 1, Type 2 Allergy Relief* (Los Angeles: Jeremy Tarcher, 1983) 118–19.

[2] Gert Behannah, "Who Is the Alcoholic?" *WEMI* radio broadcast (February 12, 1985).

[3] William Van Ornum and John Mordock, *Crisis Counseling With Children and Adolescents* (New York: Continuum, 1983) 17.

[4] William Gaylin, Ira Glasser, Steven Marcus, and David Rothman, *Doing Good: The Limits of Benevolence* (New York: Pantheon Books, 1978), 5.

[5] Frank Bruno, *Human Adjustment and Personal Growth* (New York: John Wiley & Sons, 1977), 358.

[6] Dr. William Glasser, *Control Theory—A New Explanation of How We Control Our Lives* (New York: Harper & Row, 1984), 5–15.

[7] Ibid., 24.

[8] Ibid., 26.

Desperate to Be Needed

[9] Robert Subby and John Friel, *Co-Dependency and Family Rules* (Pompano Beach, Fla.: Health Communications, Inc., 1984), 32.

[10] Kathy Capell-Sowder, "Co-Dependent Relationships," published in *Co-Dependency, A Book of Readings* reprinted from "Focus on Family and Chemical Dependency," compiled and published by the *U.S. Journal of Drugs and Alcohol Dependency* (Deerfield Beach, Fla.: Health Communications, Inc., 1988), 26.

[11] Melody Beattie, *Codependent No More* (New York: Harper/Hazeldon, 1987), 31.

[12] Jacqueline Castine, *Recovery from Rescuing* (Deerfield Beach, Fla.: Health Communications, Inc., 1989), 159.

[13] Colette Dowling, *The Cinderella Complex: Women's Hidden Fear of Independence* (New York: Summit Books, 1981), 159.

Chapter 3

[1] Jon Marmor, "Children of Alcoholics Getting a Helping Hand," *L.A. Times* (December 4, 1980), 1.

[2] Composition of notes taken from Family Education Series, Elmbrook Memorial Hospital, Brookfield, Wis.

Chapter 4

[1] "The Enabler: The Companion to Chemical Dependency," Johnson Institute publication (Minneapolis: 1979), 2.

[2] Dowling, *The Cinderella Complex*, 114.

Chapter 5

[1] "This is Al-Anon," (New York: Al-Anon Family Group Headquarters, 1967), 3–4.

[2] Alcoholics Victorious, Inter-National Headquarters, P.O. Box 10364, Portland, OR 97210.

[3] The Other Victims of Alcoholism, Inc., P.O. Box 921, Radio City Station, N.Y., N.Y. 10019.

[4] Hazelden Foundation, P.O. Box 11, Center City, MN 55012-0011.

[5] Dr. Vernon Johnson, *I'll Quit Tomorrow*, (New York: Harper & Row, 1973), 49–51.

106

Chapter 6

[1] William Gaylin, Ira Glasser, Steven Marcus, and David Rothman, *Doing Good: The Limits of Benevolence* (New York: Pantheon Books, 1978), 10.
[1] Ibid., 10.
[2] *Ibid.*, 7.
[3] *Ibid.*, 12.
[4] David A. Seamands, "Damaged Emotions" (published by Narramore Christian Foundation, 1969), 5.
[5] Dowling, *The Cinderella Complex*, back cover copy.
[6] McCabe, *Victims No More*, 56–58.

Chapter 7

[1] Martin De Haan II, "How Can I Feel Good About Myself?" a publication of Radio Bible Class Ministries (1988), 4.
[2] Dr. Dan Kiley, *The Wendy Dilemma: When Women Stop Mothering Their Men* (New York: Arbor House, 1984), 41.
[3] Subby and Friel, *Co-Dependency and Family Rules*, 46.
[4] Janet Woititz, *Adult Children of Alcoholics* (Hollywood, Fla.: Health Communications, 1983), 46–47.
[5] Glasser, *Control Theory*, 61.
[6] Gaylin, et. al., *Doing Good*, 27.
[7] Nathaniel Brandon, *Honoring the Self: Personal Integrity and the Heroic Potentials of Human Nature* (New York: Houghton Mifflin Co., 1983), 28.
[8] Dr. Robert Schuller, *Be Happy—You Are Loved* (Nashville: Thomas Nelson, Inc., 1986), 87.

Chapter 8

[1] McCabe, *Victims No More*, 36.
[2] Dr. James Dobson, *Love Must Be Tough* (Waco, Tex.: Word, Inc., 1986), 176.
[3] Schuller, *Be Happy—You Are Loved*, 203.

Chapter 10

[1] James Pittman, "What To Do With A Broken Relationship," a booklet distributed by Radio Bible Class Ministries (1978), 4.
[2] Dobson, *Love Must Be Tough*, 176.
[3] Schuller, *Be Happy—You Are Loved*, 203.

4 Subby and Friel, *Codependency and Family Rules*, 33.
5 McCabe, *Victims No More*, 58.
6 Dr. Bernard Siegel, *Love, Medicine and Miracles* (New York: Harper & Row, 1987), 198–99.

Chapter 11

1 McCabe, *Victims No More*, 93.
2 Brent Lamb, "Quiet, Please," from the album "Tug of War," (Grand Rapids: Zondervan, 1984), side 1.

Chapter 12

1 Carolyn Hoffman, "Bloom Where You Are Planted," source unknown.
2 Schuller, *Be Happy—You Are Loved*, 109–10.

BIBLIOGRAPHY

Anthony, Dr. Robert. *The Ultimate Secrets of Total Self-Confidence.* New York: Berkley Books, 1979.

Beattie, Melody. *Codependent No More.* New York: Harper/Hazelden, 1987.

Branden, Nathaniel. *Honoring the Self: Personal Integrity and the Heroic Potentials of Human Nature.* New York: Houghton Mifflin, 1983.

Castine, Jacqueline. *Recovery From Rescuing.* Deerfield Beach, Fla.: Health Communications, 1989.

————. *Codependency.* A Book of Readings reprinted from "Focus on Family and Chemical Dependency," compiled and published by the *U. S. Journal of Drug and Alcohol Dependency* and Health Communications, Inc., Deerfield Beach, Fla.: Health Communications, Inc., 1988.

Costales, Claire. *Alcoholism . . . The Way Back to Reality.* Los Angeles: Gospel Light Publications, 1980.

De Haan, Martin. "How Can I Feel Good About Myself?" *Radio Bible Class Publications,* 980.

Dobson, Dr. James. *Love Must Be Tough.* Waco, Tex.: Word, Inc., 1986.

Dowling, Colette. *The Cinderella Complex: Women's Hidden Fear of Independence.* New York: Summit Books, 1981.

————. "The Enabler: A Companion to Chemical Dependency." A Johnson Institute pamphlet. Minneapolis: Johnson Institute, 1975.

Gaylin, Dr. William, Ira Glasser, Steven Marcus, and David Rothman. *Doing Good: The Limits of Benevolence.* New York: Pantheon Books, 1978.

Glaser, Dr. William, Steven Marcus, and David Rothman. *Control Theory— A New Explanation of How We Control Our Lives.* New York: Harper & Row, 1984.

Hafen, Brent. *The Crisis Intervention Handbook.* Englewood Cliffs, N.J.: Prentice Hall, 1982.

Hazelden Foundation, P. O. Box 11, Center City, MN 55012-0011.

Johnson, Dr. Vernon. *I'll Quit Tomorrow.* New York: Harper & Row, 1973.

Desperate to Be Needed

Kiley, Dr. Dan. *The Wendy Dilemma: When Women Stop Mothering Their Men.* New York: Arbor House, 1984.

Levin, Dr. Allen and Merla Zellerback. *Type 1, Type 2 Allergy Relief.* Los Angeles: Jeremy Tarcher, 1983.

McCabe, Thomas. *Victims No More.* Center City, Minn.: Hazeldon Educational Materials, 1978.

Schuller, Dr. Robert. *Be Happy—You Are Loved.* Nashville: Thomas Nelson, Inc., 1986.

Siegel, Dr. Bernard. *Love, Medicine, and Miracles: Lessons Learned About Self-Healing From A Surgeon's Experience With Exceptional Patients.* New York: Harper & Row, 1987.

Subby, Robert and John Friel. *Codependency and Family Rules.* Pompano Beach, Fla.: Health Communications, Inc., 1984.

Van Ornum, William, and John Murdock. *Crisis Counseling With Children and Adolescents.* New York: Continuum, 1983.

Woititz, Janet G. *Adult Children of Alcoholics.* Hollywood, Fla.: Health Communications, 1983.